33008
√94

The College Learning Resource Center

Dwight F. Burlingame

Dennis C. Fields

Anthony C. Schulzetenberg

Libraries Unlimited, Inc. - Littleton, Colo. - 1978

LIBRARIES UNLIMITED, INC.
P.O. Box 263
Littleton, Colorado 80160

Library of Congress Cataloging in Publication Data

Burlingame, Dwight.
    The college learning resource center.

    Includes index.
    1. Libraries, University and college.
2. Instructional materials centers. I. Fields,
Dennis C., 1938-   joint author.
II. Schulzetenberg, Anthony C., 1929-   joint
author. III. Title.
Z675.U5B89   025.1   78-13716
ISBN 0-87287-189-4

TABLE OF CONTENTS

LIST OF ILLUSTRATIONS

To

Audrey, Anne, and Mary Jane

INTRODUCTION

The unification of all educational resource services into a single administrative unit, the college learning resource center (LRC), represents a concept novel enough so that, until now, few works concerning both its organizational philosophy and its actual administration have been published. Yet, this has remained the situation in spite of the fact that the learning resources concept includes all materials and equipment that contribute to learning, the local production facilities for the preparation of software, and those interface functions that are central in serving the academic community. Standard administration texts for college and university libraries, such as Lyle's *The Administration of the College Library*, and Rogers and Weber's *University Library Administration*, are extremely valuable in the traditional sense and remain relevant for administering some aspects of the college LRC. Works like Stueart and Eastlick's *Library Management*, and Hicks and Tillin's *Managing Multimedia Libraries*, have incorporated newer administrative concepts and expanded somewhat the scope of the traditional library. Marchant's *Participative Management in Academic Libraries*, Chisholm and Ely's *Media Personnel in Education*, Grove's *Nonprint Media in Academic Libraries*, Evans's *Management Techniques*, and Brown, Norberg, and Srygley's *Administering Educational Media* are typical of a range of books on various aspects of the academic library. Nevertheless, while all of the aforementioned books deal with some aspect of administration, none has significantly explored the entirety of the college learning resource center, including both the conceptual and organizational aspects of a truly coordinated program.

The authors have undertaken herein to establish a philosophical base that can help to both develop an organizational structure for learning resources and provide insight into the administration of such a program. Supplemented by the above-mentioned detailed works on college library and technical services administration, *The College Learning Resource Center* can serve both as a textbook on the concept in general and as a handbook for administrators of such a program. Theoretical discussions combined with actual examples help student and administrator alike to understand the principles and practices that allow for full implementation of the concept. Contrasting views are examined to provide an idea of the range of opinions on various topics concerned with the operation of the LRC. The notes and additional references provided for each chapter direct readers to materials that have proven valuable in the authors' experiences with learning resources, either as inspiration or as pragmatic aids in specific problem situations.

The book begins with a brief description of the contemporary general academic environment, since the parent institution dictates its learning center's philosophical direction and physical limitations. The second chapter presents the philosophy behind unified learning resources and discusses theorists, researchers, and practitioners. Discussion and illustration of a variety of possible general organizational patterns form Chapter 3, subsequent chapters being concerned with the various individual functional areas of the program: resources and information, instructional technology services, instructional development and faculty development, and technical services. Each of these chapters synthesizes goals and procedures for individual units, all within the learning resources philosophy and considered as part of the program in its entirety. The final chapter concerns itself with management in general, the need for clear personnel policies and how to establish them, and the options available for setting up a program's financial system. As a further convenience for users of *The College Learning Resource Center*, appendices present the ALA Resources and Technical Services Division's Collection Development Committee "Guidelines for the Formulation of Collection Development Policies" and a sampling of actual job descriptions for various positions in learning resources centers.

The authors have drawn freely upon their experiences with learning resource programs for this work, and their analysis of other programs and works in all areas of organization and administration has also been incorporated. This blend of theory and practice helps to give a balanced view when placing learning resources in perspective within the academic community.

The terms college and university have been used interchangeably in this book, as is the case in most works on higher education. (Yet, this is not to imply a necessity for immediate implementation of the learning resources concept on all academic levels, for each institution must determine whether the concept is academically feasible, cost effective, and consistent with the educational program in its entirety.) The terms library and learning resource center are also used interchangeably, for terminology in this developing area is presently less fixed than it may be when the concept is more widespread. Also, certain acronyms common to the learning resources concept have been used: LRC (learning resource center), ITS (instructional technology services), FD (faculty development), ID (instructional development), and MBO (management by objectives).

Partial support for research on this book was granted by the University of Evansville Alumni Research and Scholarly Activity Fellowships, and appreciation is expressed for that assistance. The photographs were taken at St. Cloud State University's LRC and are the work of its staff. Thanks go as well to Judy Unfried for typing the manuscript.

D.F.B.
D.C.F.
A.C.S.

1

THE COLLEGE COMMUNITY

Since the college learning resource center is inextricably intertwined with its parent institution, any work on the administration of the center must describe, however briefly, the major factors that affect the college community. It is highly desirable in any study of learning resource centers that the nature of the parent institution be clearly understood since, ideally, the objectives of a learning resource center are determined largely by the objectives of the institution of which it is a part. A more detailed look at the demands of the public, the faculty, and the students shows the changing role of today's academic community and the impact of those changes on the college resource center.

PUBLIC DEMANDS ON COLLEGES

The growing significance of higher education in the American educational system and the challenges with which that educational system is confronted have been highlighted in several reports and recommendations of the Carnegie Commission on Higher Education. In its 1968 special report, *Quality and Equality*, the Commission said:

> From the beginnings of the republic, education at various levels has played a vital role in the building of a strong democratic society. At earlier stages in the nation's development, this role was chiefly the responsibility of the primary and secondary institutions. Now, as education through high school has become almost universal and knowledge has increased, the professional intellectual demands on society have become ever more complex and exacting, their responsibility has shifted increasingly to American colleges and universities. . . . Above all, the nation and world depend crucially upon rigorous and creative ideas for the solution to profound, complex issues.[1]

The American public needs and expects from its colleges a strong academic quality if they are to meet the needs of contemporary society. Therefore, colleges must energetically and even aggressively develop new ways to meet their educational responsibilities. Yet, "the confidence of higher education in its capacity to achieve continued progress toward equality of opportunity and toward the advancement of knowledge has been shaken in the last few years by the development of an unprecedented financial crisis."[2] The Commission suggests that one solution to this crisis is the more effective use of resources. Colleges today have as their responsibility the careful analysis of the relationship between their use of resources and the attainment of their goals, the implementation of maximum economies with little sacrifice in quality, the encouragement of flexible and rapid adaptation to changes of their curriculum, and the promotion of educational public service and research programs.[3]

Pressures for reform in the American college have been relatively constant in the United States; however, the present intensity of the changing character of American society and its institutions had its origin in the post-World War II period, when a compelling need for personnel, space, educational facilities, and other resources forced colleges and universities to accommodate an unexpected increase in enrollment.[4] Because of the American college environment of the 1960s (i.e., campus disruption, abandonment of traditions, and seemingly constant demand for change), tension has become a part of the college academic atmosphere. The educational consumer has demanded specific information concerning management practices and has exposed weaknesses in campus procedures and policies. These trends have caused public suspicion about the worth of a college education, a suspicion that has not abated with a job market that continues to cause employment problems for the college graduate.

To gain an appreciation of the history of the American college and its development, it would be worthwhile for those interested in the role of the learning resource center to refer to Nevitt Sanford's classic *The American College*, or the briefer version of that work entitled *College in Character.* Although published in 1962 and 1964 respectively, these works are still most appropriate. Sanford clearly illustrates the complexity and diversity of the institution and how it is affected by various political, sociological, and economic forces in American society. He also focused upon the individual student's development under the influence of social as well as inter-psychological forces.

Many of the experimenting and innovative four-year colleges and universities covered in Ann Heiss's work have in some way adopted the organizational pattern of a learning resource center. The past decade has been a time of centralized catalogs, computerized operations, extended use of multi-media to support instruction, and various new mechanized instrumentation to expand service capabilities.[5] The college library has been and continues to be one of the primary vehicles for access to man's graphic record.[6] Even this pillar of tradition, however, has not escaped the major trends in education. One such trend is in budgeting. Library budgets can be expected to increase equally as much and perhaps even more rapidly than other expenditures. Book and periodical costs continue to increase faster than the general cost of living, while the expectations and demands of college library users have increased and changed in nature. A recent study referred to in *The Chronicle of Higher Education* substantiates this trend:

> According to the Association of Research Libraries the price of
> academic books has risen by 167 per cent since 1967. The impact of
> inflation has been so great than even those major research libraries that
> have increased their budgets are falling behind in acquisitions. . . .
> These figures parallel the data from 78 members of the Association
> of Research Libraries, which report a 36.5 per cent budgetary increase
> since 1970 but a 12.5 per cent decline in the gross number of volumes
> added per year.[7]

Access to college library resources, as well as university resources, will have to be
improved in light of changing demands that strain the capacity of single libraries
to meet the needs of their constituencies and that will necessitate more aggressive
pursuit of inter-institutional networks and systems among libraries. Further application of the new technology in storing, retrieving, and transmitting graphic records
will be demanded by institutional use.

The financial crisis in higher education is naturally of major significance to
libraries and learning centers. In this context, the organizational pattern of each
needs to be carefully examined. However, the search for effective use of resources
in college today should not be regarded purely as a response to financial complexities. Administrators and management ideally will continue to seek ways to achieve
more effective use of resources without the impetus of a financial crisis.

The change in college libraries to include all forms of media is significant in
that the addition of other types of activities has placed greater emphasis on
instructors' making full use of available resources. Learning resources professionals,
then, will become the active agent bringing together man's graphic records and the
user of them. This function will more closely align the learning resource center
with the primary function of a college, which is to provide the highest quality
education possible for its students through improved instruction and better
opportunities for independent learning.

Thus, the college library can be expected to continue to reflect the parent
institution of which it is a part. The greatest challenge facing management in
each college library today is to make the most effective allocation, justification,
and use of limited resources in relationship to the objectives of the college community. This task implies the use of tools of organization and of systems development
in planning, budget preparation, utilization, and evaluation of the resources and
activities of a college library.

Increased emphasis should be given to management consideration in library/
learning resource facility planning and space utilization. Whether to centralize or
decentralize learning resource facilities on campus ought to be a major concern
of college librarians and university administrators. This and other problems related
to the use of facilities are indeed complex and differ from institution to institution.
Facility development and space utilization are still other factors that add to the
intensity of the organizational work facing academic librarians as they strive to
meet the goals of both the college and the library.

FACULTY

The American professoriate has in recent years suffered a partial loss of esteem. A recent major study, Everett Ladd and Martin Lipsit's *The Divided Academy* (New York: McGraw-Hill, 1975), presents a well-documented portrait of the academic profession not found in the majority of works on the professoriate. This work and a review of recent articles in the professional literature clearly point toward evaluation, collective bargaining, academic freedom, job security, governance, and faculty development as some of the major concerns of faculty today.

A renewed legitimacy has been given to an emphasis on teaching. Such a judgment on the part of faculty, of course, depends upon the extent to which the local academic community subscribes to the "publish or perish" syndrome, the openness with which the faculty approaches newer teaching strategies, and the demands for educational change from students. Disenchantment with traditional methods and demands for changes in undergraduate education from young people and their parents have given further impetus to the rise of the regional university and the community college, resulting in some major setbacks for many state colleges.

Faculty bargaining became a major force in American academic governance in the late 1960s. Its influence has increased in the 1970s, and will likely continue and be modified by various models.[8] According to *The Chronicle of Higher Education*, 544 campuses during the 1976-1977 academic year chose collective bargaining agents.[9] The full impact that this movement will have upon the American college remains in question; however, the obvious trend toward adversary rather than collegial relationships between faculty and administration is certain to have a lasting effect. Librarians, counselors, and other professionals will obviously be affected as well, especially in light of their battle for faculty status. A trend toward centralized control of budgets and policies at universities, when combined with decreasing faculty input, continues to affect the organizational pattern of such institutions.

Many colleges and universities are faced with leveling student enrollment, a declining number of faculty positions, and consequently, greater numbers of tenured faculty. In order to maintain a vigorous educational environment, greater emphasis is being placed upon faculty development. Opportunities for faculty professional development have been available in the form of sabbatical leave, research grants, and travel to professional meetings. However, these traditional forms are being supplemented by various efforts to help faculty grow as teachers. With emphasis shifting toward instructional development, learning resources, teaching improvement, faculty development, and professional development, then, the need for a comprehensive learning resource center with a well-developed organizational pattern is evident.

STUDENTS

Historically college students formed a rather homogeneous group. Even with the growth in enrollments during the past one hundred years, student bodies in the early part of the century remained rather homogeneous. As a result of the influence of the "German University" concept, the lecture method was introduced into American colleges and universities. The rigid curriculum that had characterized American colleges was abandoned in favor of an elective system, and more freedom was granted to students to pursue various courses of study and select courses that they desired. This particular system was not as successful in America though; thus, in the early part of this century, methods were advocated that would insure strong curricula dependent upon one another.

Flexible arrangements have become necessary for students who pursue alternative educational tracks. Such programs permit students to acquire knowledge in an informal or formal fashion at a location and time that meets their particular needs. The pace at which the students pursue their courses of study is also flexible, geared to meet individual abilities and temperaments. However, this kind of programming also demands a large variety of freely accessible learning materials that can satisfy diverse needs.

Various elements affecting library service in the last century have resulted in an evolution from the book-centered library toward a user-centered institution. With this emphasis upon the enlargement of the library's traditional role, the general resources of the college itself have been enlarged and amplified by newer media formats. Services have been expanded, with an aim toward establishing and improving contact between the learning center and the student. Whether the facility is called a library or learning resource center seems of little consequence so long as there are complimentary academic capabilities and opportunities. The student's role as consumer advocate will most certainly be an important factor in tomorrow's academic community. Since students are the primary consumer group, it appears that they will continue to make greater demands upon the academic community as they become more adept at fulfilling the advocacy role.

THE FUTURE

Despite the mounting pressures at all levels of education for accountability, costs and benefits are extraordinarily difficult to assess. Greater curriculum flexibility will continue to have an impact; so will the role of life-long learning and alternative education. Certainly, the college learning resource center will need to be attuned to movements in this realm if it is to meet the needs such programs demand. Almost daily, the emphasis upon alternative programs or external learning programs is expanding, with a resulting increase in enrollment.

Any major change in the organizational pattern of libraries and audiovisual centers in universities and colleges requires several years of concentrated effort if the desired objectives are to be achieved. Robert Diamond, when discussing change in higher education, says: "Academic change is never easy. It is often frustrating, sometimes traumatic, and regardless of the investment, never guaranteed."[10] This is not, of course, atypical. Those who assist in such pioneering will achieve satisfaction and must be willing to take risks. Reorganizing toward a new concept and unity requires diligent, competent personnel to interrelate appropriate theories that exist between the fields. Following through in implementing such programs is equally critical. Administrators of colleges and universities can play an important role in removing barriers to change by encouraging innovation and experimentation. They may not be able to direct innovative programs to be undertaken, but they can apply pressure through budgeting, leadership, and example to encourage further innovation.

It would appear in the final analysis that many of the new reforms in higher education today have not been working well, and little serious evaluation has been made of them, either at individual institutions or comparatively among those institutions. It is evident that the vision needed for long-term planning is equally necessary in guiding day-to-day operations. Indeed, from this dual perspective of facing contemporary challenges while creating opportunity for the future this work on the organization and administration of the contemporary college learning resource center has been written.

NOTES

[1] Carnegie Commission on Higher Education, *Quality and Equality: New Levels of Federal Responsibility for Higher Education* (New York: McGraw-Hill, 1968), p. 1.

[2] Carnegie Commission on Higher Education, *The More Effective Use of Resources: An Imperative for Higher Education* (New York: McGraw-Hill, 1972), p. vii.

[3] Ibid, p. viii.

[4] Ann Heiss, *An Inventory of Academic Innovation and Reform* (Berkeley, CA: Carnegie Commission on Higher Education, 1973), p. vii.

[5] Ibid., p. 109.

[6] For an authoritative discourse on this topic, see Jesse Shera, *Foundations of Education for Librarianship* (New York: Hayes and Becker Information Science Service, 1972).

[7] Frederick S. Starr, "A New Capital of the Intellect?" *Chronicle of Higher Education* 15 (Nov. 21, 1977): 32.

[8] Kenneth P. Mortimer and Mark D. Johnson, "Faculty Collective Bargaining in Public Higher Education." *Educational Record* 57 (Winter 1976): 34-44.

[9] *Chronicle of Higher Education* 14 (May 31, 1977): 10.

[10] Robert M. Diamond, *Guide to Instructional Development for Individualized Learning in Higher Education* (Englewood Cliffs, NJ: Educational Technology Publications, 1975), p. 3.

2

CENTENNIAL HALL
LEARNING
RESOURCES
CENTER

THE PHILOSOPHY OF THE LEARNING
RESOURCE CENTER

The success of any college is determined primarily by the quality of instruction provided for its students. In recognition of the fact that each student must provide the initial response to learning, the environment in which this takes place is composed of interrelated aptitudes, abilities, desires, methods of instructions, and such other factors as may affect it. Since that learning is a highly individualized activity, the learning resource center (LRC) as described in this book places primary emphasis upon serving the many varied needs and learning styles of the students within its constituency. This chapter outlines a philosophy that will allow development of an organizational pattern for the LRC useful in meeting the demands of today's college community.

DEVELOPMENT OF CONCEPT

Administrators of colleges are frequently asked to consider proposals to integrate or combine part or all of the existing instructional support services. The rationale that centralization will result in improved administration, better planning, coordination of services, and lesser costs is frequently offered. In light of the economic pressures upon institutions of higher education, and with the emphasis on accountability, examination of learning resource centers is warranted as well. Further, it should be understood that the integration of all available media formats is for the benefit of present as well as potential users.[1]

The establishment of the concept of learning resources in higher education is a recent development. In its 1972 report *The Fourth Revolution*, the Carnegie Commission appropriately noted:

> Efforts to free libraries from the restraints of a totally print oriented mission have been underway for many years. The advent of electronic media and new interests in instructional technology have reinforced this interest. One of the main reasons for change in attitudes on this subject on the nation's campuses has been a realization that the

25

resources of campus libraries (now frequently called information
centers or learning resource centers) have been inadequately utilized
in the instructional effort of colleges and universities.[2]

The greatest acceptance in higher education for this concept has been in the
junior or community colleges. The "AAJC-ACRL Guidelines for Two-Year College Learning Resources Programs" are supportive of learning resource programs.[3]
Additionally, Kenneth Allen and Loran Allen in their book *Organization and
Administration of the Learning Resource Centers in the Community College* have
as their focus the administration of LRCs in the community college. Fritz Veit, in
his work on *The Community College Library* (1975), also emphasized the concept
of the LRC, although he chose the shorter word "library" to use in the title of his
work. As stated in its preface, his book is addressed to "the student of the community college and its learning resource program: to community college learning
resource center staff who may wish to compare their goals and practices with those
of other institutions. . . ."[4] Max Raines, in his survey of developmental trends in
libraries and learning resource centers, noted that approximately three out of four
reporting colleges had integrated their libraries and learning resources by 1973.

That the concept has been fairly well accepted by a majority of public schools
is evidenced by the ALA-NEA *Standards* set forth for school media programs.[5]
While higher education need not model itself after public schools, the advent of the
media center and the student's work in it do have implications when the student
then enters institutions of higher learning.

Especially significant to the development of the role of the learning resource
center in the four-year college has been the publication of *The Fourth Revolution*
and statements by other bodies that deal with higher education. Librarians and
audiovisualists are actively examining the concept of learning resources envisioned
by the Carnegie Commission in this document. The publication itself states:

> The Carnegie Commission believes that the library by whatever
> name should occupy a central role in the instructional resources of
> educational institutions. Its personnel should be available not only for
> guidance to materials held in the collections of the campus, but also
> should, when qualified by subject matter expertise, be utilized as instruc-
> tors. We also believe that non-print information, illustrations, and
> instructional software components should be maintained as part of a
> unified information-instructional resource that is cataloged and stored
> in ways that facilitate convenient retrieval as needed by students and
> faculty members.[6]

The Minnesota Higher Education Coordinating Commission, in its report
Responding to Change, suggested that one way to achieve more effective use of
resources is to achieve better utilization of physical facilities.[7] One way to do this
is by combining the traditionally separate library and audiovisual units into one
learning resource unit. Greater utilization of space and manpower theoretically
should contribute to more effective use of resources.

An important advantage often mentioned as beneficial to the learning resource
organization is the ability to facilitate the efficient use of all resources by the students. When a learning environment makes all forms of materials centrally accessible,

it is argued that patrons can use them with greater efficiency. Certainly, much can be said for the concept that the contents supersede the package in importance. Therefore, it seems of little importance whether the message is delivered in the form of a book, a slide, a film, a computer program, or whatever format the writer or producer chooses.

Little disagreement currently exists as to the value of and need for providing resources other than the printed page. The traditional problem has been in defining what the LRC really is, what it should encompass, and how it relates to the campus community. The authors hold that the learning resource concept embodies all materials and equipment that contribute to learning, local production facilities for the preparation of software, and interface functions central in serving the academic community.

Although learning resource centers in senior colleges have been growing at a much slower rate than in junior colleges and secondary schools, it appears that the senior college library is moving from a passive to an active role in the processes of learning and teaching. In 1968, Sidney Forman's survey of 1,193 college libraries indicated that 10 percent of the libraries were involved in implementing some aspect of the learning resources concept, and 37 percent were planning to introduce part of the concept in the future.[8]

The learning resource center cannot be a passive agent within the institution. It must be catalytic and ever changing. As is obvious from even a superficial examination, the traditional library and the traditional audiovisual center are changing gradually, and various organizational mutations are taking place. In order for any center to have its greatest impact and to make positive contributions, it must be harmonious within the institution it serves. Success can well result from an integration of services; however, total success will only be realized when needed services—both traditional and nontraditional—are actually provided to students and faculty. Only through cooperative efforts will the contributions of the learning resource center achieve their potential.

THEORISTS

With the development of the concept of the "generic book," a term attributed mostly to Louis Shores, the seeds for further expansion of the learning resource concept were planted. Shores attributed the germination of combined library and audiovisual programs in colleges to the Carnegie Corporation, since, in 1928, it offered financial assistance to colleges to purchase phonograph records.[9] The records were intended to augment print collections by further developing audiovisual materials. In 1935, Shores introduced at George Peabody College, the first audiovisual course ever offered in the South and the first ever offered in a library school.[10]

With the publication of Shores's "AV Dimensions for an Academic Library" in 1954, the foundations were laid for an active dialogue between librarians and audiovisualists about the concept of combining their respective materials.[11] By 1955, the debate had carried itself to the pages of *Educational Screen*, where Professors Shores[12] and L. C. Larson[13] stated their respective positions. Larson was in favor of maintaining independent library and audiovisual units, whereas Shores favored a unified "materials center."

Separationists argued that audiovisualists and librarians required different preparation and qualifications. Few individuals, it was felt, could combine the two vast areas of specialization into one entity. A dual system, it was suggested, allowed each specialist to master his own area, to perform a "unique" function, and thereby offer a highly specialized service. Proponents of unity, on the other hand, argued that to maintain separate units for handling book and nonbook materials was neither logical nor efficient. After all, they countered, the first books were in fact audiovisual materials (i.e., clay tablets and pictographs), and the first integration of print and nonprint is often traced back to the first picture book, *Orbis Pictus.*[14]

Edgar Dale is another theorist of importance since his "cone of experience" and other ideas have contributed to the development of the learning resources concept. In 1953, Dale viewed the library as going through a transitional phase, stating that "It is shifting from being a repository of ideas in print to a repository of ideas on film, on tape."[15] C. Walter Stone, a strong proponent of unification of book and nonbook materials, also has stated that the most efficient library for use by student and teacher, as well as the most efficient to administer, is one that utilizes a cross-media approach.[16]

Finally, in this matter, many audiovisualists and librarians (as Dale has for many years) have come to quote Vespasiano's comments about a wealthy Italian of the fifteenth century:

> We come now to consider in what high esteem the Duke [Frederigo, Duke of Urbino, 1422-1482] held all Greek and Latin writers, sacred as well as secular. He alone had a mind to do what no one had done for a thousand years or more; that is, to create the finest library since ancient times. He spared neither cost nor labour, and when he knew of a fine book, whether in Italy or not, he would send for it. It is now fourteen or more years ago since he began the library, and he always employed, in Urbino, in Florence and in other places, thirty or forty scribes in his services. . . . In this library all the books are superlatively good, and written with the pen, and had there been one printed volume it would have been ashamed in such company.[17]

RESEARCHERS

Few completed research studies deal with the learning resources concept in higher education. One of the earlier studies that deal with the problem areas in adopting an LRC approach was Trevor Duprey's *Ferment in College Libraries* (1968). In this study, he identified three principal problem areas:

1. The first concerns structure, coordination of activities, and functional relationships within the learning resources center and other activities on the campus.
2. The proper use and coordination of non-book media with book media in the learning process.
3. There are few trained specialists who are also good managers with knowledge, experience and understanding of both areas.[18]

Also, in 1968, Duprey's study of college libraries identified the idea of accountability inherent within the philosophy of a single administrative unit and indicated that there seemed to be duplication of effort and unnecessary competition between instructional technologists and librarians.[19]

Robert Brundin's research surveyed the learning resource center development on the junior college campus.[20] Utilizing the historical method as well as the case study, he concluded that the development of learning resource centers in junior colleges was one attempt to make the library the "heart of the campus."

Richard Vorwerk examined the environmental demands and organizational status of academic libraries.[21] He found that the exclusion of newer forms of media from some academic libraries could be caused by a desire on the part of administrators to avoid materials that brought them uncertainties regarding their work (e.g., how should the nonprint materials be organized? What is the proper role of such materials in the academic library?).

John Ellison's research represented the first study of learning resource centers as such on college and university campuses.[22] Using a questionnaire and the case study method with the interview technique at selected institutions of a national sample, he identified principles that validate the concept of an integrated learning resource center on a university or college campus. The thirteen principles that reached statistical significance using the Kruskal-Wallis text were the following:

Print and nonprint materials should be cataloged according to one classification scheme.

One facility should have all print and nonprint materials.

Faculty and students are better served by one facility housing print, nonprint materials and equipment.

Print and nonprint materials should be intershelved when possible.

Print, nonprint materials and equipment should be available to students and faculty for the same number of hours.

Professional staff should be assigned some responsibilities in both print and nonprint.

One budget should be allocated for all print and nonprint materials and equipment.

The director of the learning resource center should have the ultimate responsibility for determining the departmental budget within the center.

There should be a single charging system for all print and nonprint materials.

There should be a single booking system for all print and nonprint materials.

There should be a single reserve collection for all print and nonprint materials.

All distribution and retrieval of print, nonprint materials and equipment should be centralized.

(Quote continues on page 30.)

Both print and nonprint materials and equipment should be under one administrator.[23]

PRACTITIONERS

In order for a library to consider offering audiovisual services, Donald Ely made it clear, one must first know who will be served, with what information needs, for what objectives and why.[24] He saw the use of media and technology as an evolution taking place in the contemporary college library.

Richard Taylor, Richard Ducote, and Johnny Wheelbarger spoke to the transition taking place in today's academic library (i.e., integrating the library and audiovisual services into one functional unit). The writings of all of the above authors support Wheelbarger in his 1973 statement that the LRC concept has the following implications for the operation of the combined media program:

1. There is a greater flexibility in the utilization of budgets, staff and facilities.
2. Total coordination of all elements can be called upon in the solution of learning problems.
3. The traditional emphasis on library science may give way to a variety of meaningful activities.
4. The traditional emphasis on book storage and protection may shift to an emphasis on service.
5. The learner should be the center of attention.[25]

James Holly echoed the philosophy of Shores when he stated that he (Holly) was responsible for the operation, development, and exploration of a "generic library" at Evergreen State College. By generic he meant "man's recorded information, knowledge, folly, and wisdom in whatever form put down, whether in conventional print, art forms, . . . magnetic tape, laser storage, etc."[26] In addition, Holly saw physical boundaries as inappropriate for the concept of the generic library.

Various authors have discussed how they have integrated all forms of media in one administrative unit. Some of the notable examples discussed in the literature are at St. Cloud State University, the University of Wisconsin–Stevens Point, and Oral Roberts University. Frederich Kremple notes, though, that ultimately the academic library "is faced with the necessity of working out its own policies and procedures."[27]

In an editorial in 1973, Morell Boone pointed out the example of a director of learning services (one of many names for the person formerly titled audiovisual director) who was asked about the relationship between the college library and the learning center; he answered "that he was not aware of any direct relationship. The two agencies seem to have different purposes."[28] This administrator depicted the learning center's function as an active and direct one, while he saw the library as a passive, storehouse operation. Boone concluded his editorial by noting that among the many divergent attitudes in educational and library circles he saw a polarization of thought at the two ends of the spectrum.

An attitudinal gamut from mystical devotion to atheistic skepticism exists concerning the learning resources center concept. Continued resistance to the integration of "media" services by many librarians and educational technologists suggests that the problem is how to convince skeptics that "one god is now revealed as having several persons."[29] Conflict and challenge are key ingredients from which self-confidence is built. Reorienting ourselves to the idea that media service begins with an attitude will be a major step toward bringing the concept of learning resources to fruition.

For a review of the important British literature on library resource centers, Norman Beswick's article is excellent.[30] Also of significance is the following policy statement issued by the [British] Library Association for school and college library resource centers:

> Four main questions arise concerning the exploitation of audio-visual materials in universities: production, storage, identification and provision for use. Production is most efficiently carried out by an AV unit and departments in collaboration; if the AV unit is not an independent unit, it may be administratively useful to place it under the over-all supervision of the librarian. Material may be stored in the AV unit, the library or appropriate department, depending on its intended use. It is important that material, wherever stored in the university, or available from outside sources, should be centrally recorded in the library, both for identification purposes and to avoid unnecessary duplication. Material should be provided where it can be best used, whether in department, AV unit, or library; the library is uniquely placed to handle almost all the self-instructional material, which has much in common with books, and may be used in conjunction with them. Viewing and listening equipment must, of course, be provided; some of it may be suitable for lending with the relevant software.[31]

Finally, it is appropriate to note the importance of the concept of "nontraditional study" and its impact upon the concept of learning resources. Walton pointed out that, in keeping with the trends toward external degrees, continued education as a life-long process, open universities, etc., it was necessary to create "new educational patterns that fit the times and to find creative ways in which to make available instructional resources to build programs."[32] This idea has been a factor in how senior colleges have chosen to organize the service units on their campuses. Proponents of the learning resource concept suggest that, by combining audiovisual and library services, one is in fact creating a new educational pattern that will meet the needs of students to a greater degree than present, separate organizational patterns.

William Mahler, in his review of the literature of non-traditional studies, pointed out that, of the various institutions that could provide the greatest opportunity for non-traditional study, libraries appeared to be in the best position; they were "readily available, well accepted in their communities, well staffed with professionals, and apparently willing to take on the task."[33] Attached to his study was an annotated bibliography of 263 references that would be helpful for anyone interested in further examination of this related area.

SUMMARY

In this chapter, various philosophies for integrating audiovisual and library services under a single administrative unit, the LRC, have been explored. From these has developed a view in which the center exists to serve the academic community by integrating all forms of material, providing the necessary services through a single administrative unit. All formats of media are organized and administered through this unit. It should be understood that no one model can be promulgated as the panacea for all, since local situations and service philosophies will modify the various guidelines set forth in this work. Sound judgments and implementation of learning resource programs are needed. Through the course of the remaining chapters, the organizational plan of integrated services will be emphasized in discussing various components of the learning resources organization.

NOTES

[1] Pearce S. Grove, ed. *Nonprint Media in Academic Libraries* (Chicago: American Library Association, 1975), p. x.

[2] The Carnegie Commission on Higher Education, *The Fourth Revolution: Instructional Technology in Higher Education* (New York: McGraw-Hill, 1972), p. 33.

[3] "AAJC-ACRL Guidelines for Two-Year College Library Learning Resource Centers," *College and Research Libraries News* 33 (Dec. 1972): 305-315.

[4] Fritz Veit, *The Community College Library* (Westport, CT: Greenwood Press, 1975), p. xiv.

[5] American Library Association and the National Education Association, *Standards for School Media Programs* (Chicago: ALA, 1969) and *Media Programs: District and School* (Chicago: ALA, 1975).

[6] Carnegie Commission, *The Fourth Revolution*, pp. 33-34.

[7] Minnesota Higher Education Coordinating Commission, *Responding to Change: Recommended State Policy for Meeting Minnesota's Present and Future Needs for Post-Secondary Education* (St. Paul, MN: the author, 1973), p. 14.

[8] Sidney Forman, "Innovative Practices in the College Library," *College and Research Libraries* 29 (Nov. 1968): 486.

[9] Interview with Louis Shores, Florida State University, Tallahassee, Florida, May 28, 1974.

[10] Louis Shores, *Audiovisual Librarianship: The Crusade for Media Unity* (Littleton, CO: Libraries Unlimited, Inc., 1973), p. 11.

[11] Louis Shores, "Audio-Visual Dimensions for an Academic Library," *College and Research Libraries* 15 (Oct. 1954): 393-97.

[12] Louis Shores, "Union Now: The AV Way and the Library Way," *Educational Screen: The Audio-Visual Magazine* 34 (March 1955): 112-15.

[13] L. C. Larson, "Coordinate the A-V Way and the Library Way," *Educational Screen: The Audio-Visual Magazine* 34 (Summer 1955): 252-53, 267-69.

[14] John Amos Comenius, *The Orbis Pictus* (Syracuse, NY: C. W. Bardeen, 1887).

[15] Edgar Dale, "The Challenge of Audio-Visual Media," in *Challenges to Librarianship*, ed. Louis Shores (Tallahassee, FL: Florida State University, 1953), p. 105.

[16] C. Walter Stone, "The Place of New Media in the Undergraduate Program," *Library Quarterly* 24 (Oct. 1954): 359.

[17] Vespasiano Da Bisticci, *The Vespasiano Memoirs: Lives of Illustrious Men of the XVth Century*, tr. William George and Emily Waters (London: George Routledge & Sons, Ltd., 1926), pp. 102-104.

[18] Trevor N. Duprey, *Ferment in College Libraries: The Impact of Information Technology* (Washington: Communication Service Corporation, 1968), p. 59.

[19] Trevor N. Duprey, *Modern Libraries for Modern Colleges* (Washington: Communication Service Corporation, 1968), p. 48.

[20] Robert Brundin, "Changing Patterns of Library Service in Five California Junior Colleges" (Ph.D. dissertation, Stanford University, 1970).

[21] Richard J. Vorwerk, "The Environmental Demands and Organizational Status of Two Academic Libraries" (Ph.D. dissertation, Indiana University, 1970).

[22] John William Ellison, "The Identification and Examination of Principles Which Validate or Refute the Concept of College or University Learning Resources Centers" (Ph.D. dissertation, The Ohio State University, 1972).

[23] Ibid., pp. 212-13.

[24] Donald P. Ely, "The Contemporary College Library: Change by Evolution or Revolution?" *Educational Technology* 11 (May 1971): 18.

[25] Johnny J. Wheelbarger, "The Learning Resource Center at the Four-Year College Level," *Audiovisual Instruction* 18 (March 1973): 89.

[26] James F. Holly, "The New Evergreen State College Library: Basic Assumptions," *PNLA Quarterly* 34 (Winter 1970): 21.

[27] Frederich A. Kremple, "Handling Audiovisuals in an Academic Library," *Wisconsin Library Bulletin* 66 (March-April 1970): 91.

[28] Morell D. Boone, "Camelot . . . A Quest or a Kingdom?" *College and Research Libraries* 34 (Jan. 1973): 5.

[29] Deirdre Boyle, "In the Beginning Was the Word . . . Libraries and Media," *Library Journal* 101 (Jan. 1, 1976): 126.

[30] Norman Beswick, "Library Resource Centres: A Developing Literature," *Journal of Librarianship* 6 (Jan. 1974): 54-62.

[31] "University Libraries and Learning Resources," *Library Association Record* 75 (Jan. 1973): 8.

[32] Wesley W. Walton, *New Paths for Adult Learning: Systems for the Delivery of Non-Traditional Studies* (Berkeley, CA: Educational Testing Service, 1973), p. 30.

[33] William A. Mahler, *Non-Traditional Study: A Critical Review of the Literature* (Berkeley, CA: Educational Testing Service, 1973).

3

ADMINISTRATIVE ORGANIZATION

The organizational structure of a learning resource program depends on many factors. Certainly the historical development of an institution often has a long-lasting impact upon its established pattern of organization even after the basis for such a pattern has disappeared. In that sense, the size of the institution has affected and will continue to affect its organizational pattern. Generally, the larger the institution, the more administrative levels one can expect, not only within the institution, but also within learning resources.

The general administrative philosophy of the college to which learning resources must conform also will affect the internal organization of that unit. Personnel changes in various administrative positions, then, will most naturally have a continued effect on the administrative organizational pattern. The administrative style and philosophy of people or groups in policy-making positions are usually adapted or retained from experiences at other institutions and implemented in new settings.

A third major factor, the impact of exterior regulations (state laws, commission guidelines, governing body rules, federal laws and guidelines, and similar outside forces) must not be overlooked. Such regulations have an effect upon the organizational framework since they, in fact, establish bounds and procedures in either a participatory or regulatory manner.

The educational role that the learning resources center is expected to fulfill and the dedication to this role by both the director and the entire staff will be significant in shaping the organization. For purposes of this work, learning resources is defined as a single administrative unit that includes both the library and audiovisual programs on a college campus. This unit may include any or all of the following: graphics, photography, cinematography, curriculum center, dial access, radio station, computer center, closed-circuit television, and instructional technology.

Development of the learning resources concept is not in any way a revolutionary move in education. Rather, it is an administrative combination of services and resources that have long been part of the educational environment. Libraries are continually being forced to place greater emphasis on nonprint media and to react to requests and services demanded by a wide variety of patrons. Concurrently, as technology in the communications field has developed, the audiovisual services component, often independently, has grown dramatically. Along with these developments, education has seen a renewed emphasis upon individualized instruction, which has precipitated a greater need for LRCs. With the stimulus of large sums of federal money, a strong combination of audiovisual and library services has developed.

Included in this development was an increased emphasis on local production of instructional material, which resulted in the need for a more systematic approach to instructional units and courses. Subsequently, the demand for instructional development and learning activity services increased considerably.

Gary Peterson has analyzed the learning center as a four-part amalgamation of audiovisual, library, instructional development, and non-traditional services. His rationale for such a center is based upon the following six major purposes:

1. The Learning Center provides service for faculty and students; this service supports the expressed needs of the L.C.'s patrons and so provides resources which in themselves should expand the potentials and expectancies of patrons by suggesting new avenues for learning.

2. The Learning Center provides a variety of individualized and individual experiences for patrons through independent study, media resources, tutorial activity, etc.

3. The Learning Center through a variety of services supports the instructional program offered by academic areas. In special cases where course format, such as independent studies, or subject matter relating to the Learning Center itself, or for courses which by their nature may be more easily offered via the low-cost channel of independent study, the center may itself offer courses.

4. The Learning Center provides leadership in the area of media, helping the faculty with evaluation, selection, and utilization of media appropriate to a variety of learning needs.

5. The Learning Center is concerned with learning as both a process and a product. The LC is particularly concerned with providing ways for students to become more effective learners in conventional classes, in independent study, and in the lifelong pursuit of learning.

6. The Learning Center is concerned with change and experimentation as vital forces on the campus. The Center collects and disseminates educational ideas from outside the school to personnel for their consideration and possible adoption.[1]

Peterson's rationale quite adequately reflects what has been incorporated into the learning resources concept in most institutions where it has been implemented. With a fully integrated and coordinated program designed to meet the educational demands of the patron, learning resources should be able to eliminate the dichotomous philosophical split between the traditional librarian and the traditional audiovisualist. Once a harmonious philosophical base has been established, a concentrated effort on staff development, facility planning, and program implementation can be initiated.

In 1973, McAnnally and Downs examined the role of the directors of large university libraries, suggesting possible solutions for the recent turnover and mounting pressures in such institutions. Several of those suggestions are significant and relevant to the LRC. They include, among others, organizational changes responsive to need, emphasis on service, planning that is realistic and fair, and improved budgeting.[2] Although the LRC is usually identified with smaller colleges and universities where research and publication pressures have not been as great for the chief administrator and faculty, adequate attention given to the crucial areas mentioned above should produce a properly functioning LRC in any setting. If a learning resource organizational pattern is to be effective in meeting the learning needs of its constituents, the following items should be considered:

1.   Comprehensive coordination. All media elements centralized to meet learning needs. A one-level decision-making structure is not presupposed. Decision making occurs at all levels and reflects the best professional expertise in each area of operation. Coordination is needed, however, when decisions start crossing lines of competency; likewise, it is equally important in establishing priorities when budgeting for space and utilization of scarce resources.

2.   Budget flexibility. Within a unified media program, greater flexibility in budget allocations is possible. It is not necessary to create one gigantic budget, which may be more susceptible to being cut by higher budgetary authorities. Control of the budget by the dean of learning resources can still be exercised with flexibility by maintaining separate budget allocations for individual units (i.e., library book budget, instructional production budget, etc.). The total of the center's budget, in relationship to the total institutional budget, can still be fair and can reflect a proper commitment to providing the fullest resources possible.

3.   Professional staff. Often the objection to a learning resource concept is based upon the fact that an organization of generalists rather than specialists will be created. This need not be the case. Moreover, learning resources should promote both the hybrid generalist and the specialist. For example, trained catalogers in technical processing are essential; and just as important, production specialists in administering audiovisual services are a vital component in developing learning materials.

4.   Resources. With the ever-increasing presence of a variety of media in the world, an equal variety of learning alternatives are required. One set of texts for a lecture-oriented class, one set of projects, one set of papers, or one form of research is no longer acceptable for quality instruction. Diversity of formats is necessary and must be provided if the LRC's personnel truly believe that learning takes place through visual, oral, kinetic, and other stimuli. That a learner responds at different times in different ways and at different places demands that he or she be exposed to ideas in many formats. A multi-media collection provides an instructor with the kinds of resources necessary for communicating concepts and provides students with motivation to obtain the desired learning results. The book collection naturally remains an integral part of the LRC, but the entire collection will be enhanced by the

presence of nonprint materials. There need be little concern, if these are made available, that the heretofore primary collection of nonprint materials will get second billing to print materials within the ideal resource and information collection.

5. Environment conducive to learning. Needless to say, physical surroundings—space, furniture, lighting, temperature, and aesthetics—are essential for a proper learning atmosphere. Provision for small group, large group, and individual study must be provided. Likewise, adequate electrical capabilities, wet carrels, dry carrels, audio-tutorial rooms, viewing rooms, dark rooms, or any other user requirements, whether small or large, are all components that can assist in providing an environment conducive to learning.

6. Commitment. Without a *commitment* to a total service concept, both internally and externally, the LRC has little chance of success under any organizational structure. Only through this commitment will a change in the services that are provided come about; and, consequently, only through change will all of the resources necessary for the pursuit of learning become a part of the academic environment.

Little doubt exists that junior colleges or community colleges have been the leaders in advancing the LRC in higher education. The four-year colleges and universities have been slow to accept this concept, but now some institutions are moving toward acceptance and implementation at a faster pace. The emphasis upon improvement of instruction and faculty development has produced stronger calls for consolidated programs, ones that provide total media support. The provision of such total media support for instructors also opens avenues of learning to students that they often had not had available in the academic world.

The service priority of meeting user needs has become a clarion call within the LRC movement, and every effort should be made to achieve this in the most effective and efficient manner. One way to expedite service to the user is to set up an efficient organizational structure, one directed to meeting user needs and to doing so effectively. A close look at both theoretical models and existing models will enable the reader to develop an overview of possible organizational structures, which can help to initiate thinking about possible directions.

ORGANIZATIONAL PATTERNS

In an earlier work, Burlingame and Schulzetenberg depicted a theoretical organizational chart of a learning resources center (Figure 1). One will note that the divisions in this organizational chart develop units on the basis of service rather than types of materials. The "generic book" concept prevails, and certainly it is in line with Louis Shores's notion of communicability.

Figure 1
Theoretical LRC Organizational Chart

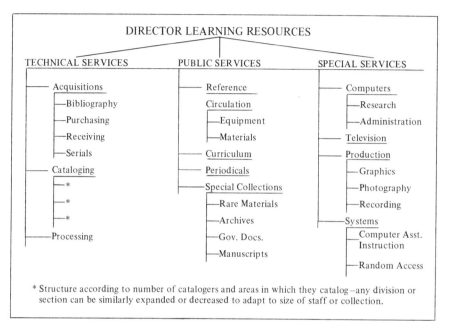

DIRECTOR LEARNING RESOURCES

TECHNICAL SERVICES	PUBLIC SERVICES	SPECIAL SERVICES
Acquisitions	Reference	Computers
—Bibliography	Circulation	—Research
—Purchasing	—Equipment	—Administration
—Receiving	—Materials	Television
—Serials	Curriculum	Production
Cataloging	Periodicals	—Graphics
—*	Special Collections	—Photography
—*	—Rare Materials	—Recording
—*	—Archives	Systems
Processing	—Gov. Docs.	Computer Asst. Instruction
	—Manuscripts	—Random Access

* Structure according to number of catalogers and areas in which they catalog—any division or section can be similarly expanded or decreased to adapt to size of staff or collection.

Source: Anthony Schulzetenberg and Dwight Burlingame, "Bringing It All Together," *Learning Today* 6 (Summer 1973), p. 71. Used by permission.

In an organization as depicted in Figure 1, different media are handled by assigning them to personnel in service units. The technical services unit, for example, would handle the processing of all formats. Acquisitions would order not only books and other print materials, but also films, periodicals, and other non-print items. Circulation, to take the concept one step further, would assume responsibility for the distribution of all media and equipment on a campus-wide basis. The learning resource organizational structure, then, is one application of a management systems approach. The charts in this chapter are designed to bring an organization's performance to its maximum efficiency. The reader should keep foremost this concept of combining like services as attention shifts from a theoretical organization to patterns that actually exist on several academic campuses today.

As a matter of principle, it is desirable that the director of the learning resource center report to the highest possible official on the campus; this will vary, of course, with each institution. In the sample organizational charts depicted in the following pages, the chief administrator of the LRC reports to the vice-president for academic affairs (or dean, the term often used for this position at smaller colleges). The trend for the head of learning resources to report to the officer in charge of academic affairs is reflected in the 1975 ACRL *Standards for College Libraries*, which state that the chief administrator "shall report to the president or the chief academic officer of the institution."[3]

The authors firmly believe that in order to achieve the necessary close contact and interaction with the instructional program of the college, it is essential that the director report to the chief officer in charge of academic affairs and *not* to some other officer in the college or university. Historically, the director reported to the head of the institution. Instances of this pattern have not been so evident in recent years, however, and it is now the exception. This is not to say that significant informal relationships do not exist between the chief administrative officer of the college and the head of the LRC. Such relationships are, of course, important in order to maintain administrative contacts that are vital to the welfare of the LRC and to the college.

At the University of Evansville (Figure 2) and at Eastern Michigan University (Figure 3), learning resources is divided into three main units. The public services division includes reference, circulation of print and nonprint materials, instruction, and other patron services. The technical services department is responsible for acquisitions and cataloging of all print and nonprint materials. The instructional services or media services unit has primary responsibility for a major portion of what formerly constituted a traditional audiovisual department.

Figure 2

**University of Evansville Learning Resources
Organizational Chart**

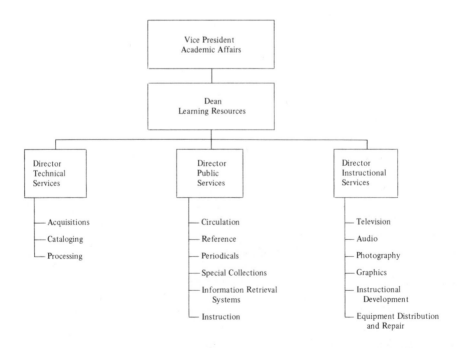

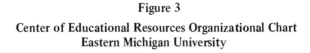

Figure 3

Center of Educational Resources Organizational Chart
Eastern Michigan University

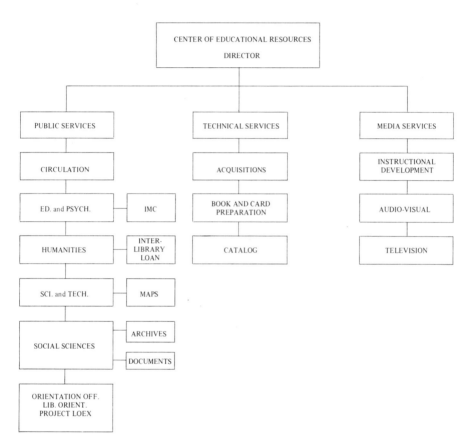

The charts for St. Cloud State University (Figure 4, page 44) and the University of Wisconsin—Stout (Figure 5, page 45) are of significance since they illustrate the combination of a service unit with an academic department. Figure 6 (page 46) and Figure 7 (page 47) provide a detailed breakdown of the University of Wisconsin—Stout's two divisions that comprise much of what is found in separate audiovisual and library divisions. This division recognizes the need for specialists, and certainly the structure does not call for an elimination of traditional roles. Catalogers, reference librarians, tele-production managers, and others are vital to fulfilling the goals of each division.

Figure 4
Learning Resources Services
St. Cloud State University, Minnesota

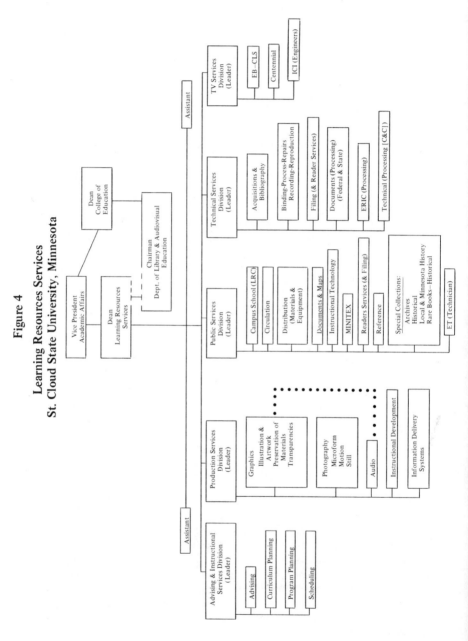

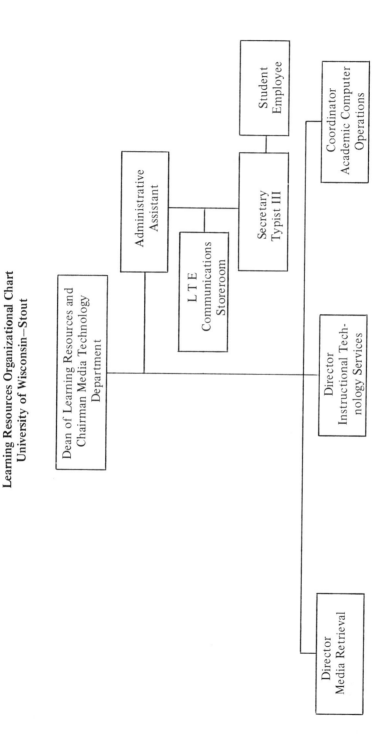

Figure 5
Learning Resources Organizational Chart
University of Wisconsin—Stout

Figure 6
Instructional Technology Services
University of Wisconsin–Stout

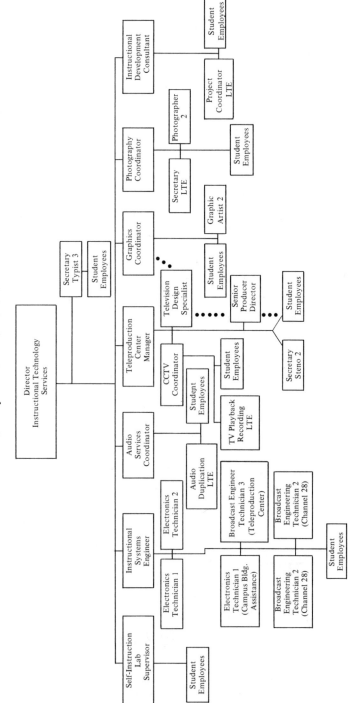

Figure 7
Media Retrieval Services
University of Wisconsin—Stout

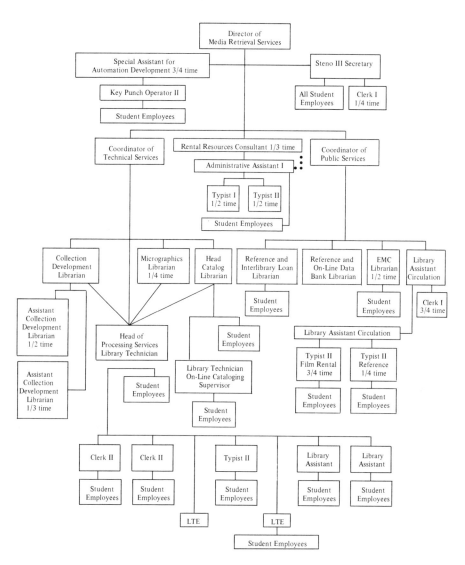

At De Anza College (Cupertino, California), the learning center (Figure 8 below, and Figure 9 on page 49) is organized to emphasize the concept that it is an attempt to marshall all of the communication media to assist learners and faculty in their pursuits. Materials, programs, and people are coordinated for maximum utilization of all resources.

Figure 8

**The Learning Center Concept at De Anza College,
Cupertino, California—"The Learning Center
Is a Learner Center"**

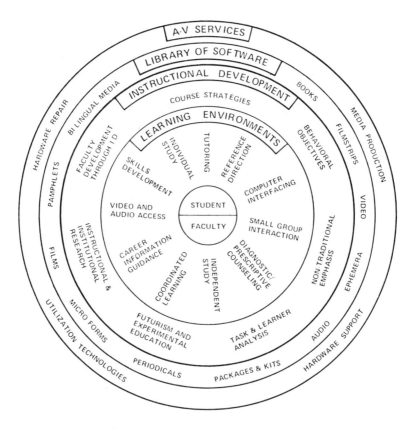

Source: Gary T. Peterson, *The Learning Center: A Sphere for Nontraditional Approaches to Education* (Hamden, CT: Linnet Books, 1975), p. 17. Used by permission.

Figure 9

Learning Center Organizational Chart
De Anza College, Cupertino, California

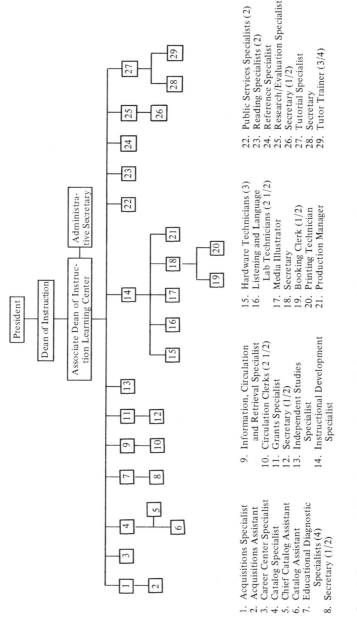

1. Acquisitions Specialist
2. Acquisitions Assistant
3. Career Center Specialist
4. Catalog Specialist
5. Chief Catalog Assistant
6. Catalog Assistant
7. Educational Diagnostic
   Specialists (4)
8. Secretary (1/2)

9. Information, Circulation
   and Retrieval Specialist
10. Circulation Clerks (2 1/2)
11. Grants Specialist
12. Secretary (1/2)
13. Independent Studies
    Specialist
14. Instructional Development
    Specialist

15. Hardware Technicians (3)
16. Listening and Language
    Lab Technicians (2 1/2)
17. Media Illustrator
18. Secretary
19. Booking Clerk (1/2)
20. Printing Technician
21. Production Manager

22. Public Services Specialists (2)
23. Reading Specialists (2)
24. Reference Specialist
25. Research/Evaluation Specialist
26. Secretary (1/2)
27. Tutorial Specialist
28. Secretary
29. Tutor Trainer (3/4)

Source: Gary T. Peterson, *The Learning Center: A Sphere for Nontraditional Approaches to Education* (Hamden, CT: Linnet Books, 1975), p. 19. Used by permission.

In summary, it can be quite readily seen that the types of organizational structures differ from institution to institution, and this undoubtedly reflects the uniqueness of each institution's basic goals within learning resources. There do appear to be some common elements apparent in all of them, and each certainly reflects a great deal of thought toward making its particular structure functional. Generally accepted guidelines for organization are apparent (such as line and staff, accountability, undue proliferation of functions, etc.) and underlying all of them is an attempt to develop a disregard for format as a determining factor. At first glance, it might appear that traditional lines have been followed through the use of traditional terms like public services, technical services, instructional services, or audiovisual services. Indeed, it may appear that the adage of old wine in new skins has been followed, but closer examination will reveal that very few of the patterns are only the traditional audiovisual and library concept with new names.

Without purporting it to be a panacea for organizational development, a structure can be presented that considers the functions that the authors feel form a basic framework for organizational development. It is based on their experience and on their study of various organizational patterns, with a view toward functional relationships and the avoidance of excessive administrative bureaucracy. A hypothetical structure as suggested in Figure 10 might provide those interested in learning resources organization with a starting point. In actuality, it is a revision of the organizational structure by Burlingame and Schulzetenberg that appears as Figure 1 (page 41).

As pointed out, the organizational structure in Figure 10 is hypothetical, but it is one in which the authors have confidence. It is a simple structure, open to expansion and free from excessive administrative overlap. A cursory look at the structure might leave the reader feeling that it is somewhat superficial. However, the authors believe that to try to include in the chart every relationship within an organization is not only impossible, but also limiting in that the plan becomes incomprehensible for those who must try to interpret it. An organizational chart that will allow the replacement of organizational titles with names or pictures of individuals is more meaningful for the interpreter than a highly complex one that tries to show each and every interrelationship. G. Edward Evans has pointed out the value of the organizational chart in his work:

> The organizational chart is a useful management tool if it is kept
> up to date. It gives a clear picture of the formal lines of communication.
> . . . The real flow of authority and decision making may differ from
> the chart, but the organizational chart is a good starting point for a new
> staff member to learn about a new institution. So many new names and
> faces in a day or two is too much for most people to handle. A chart
> with names and pictures of office holders can reduce the embarrass-
> ment and anxiety that often result, thus making the training/orienta-
> tion process more enjoyable.[4]

Figure 10
Suggested LRC Organizational Chart

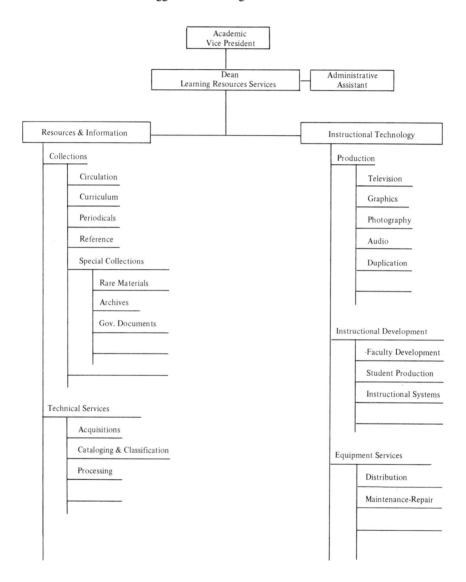

Despite its simplicity, the structure is quite open to expansion, since each division or subdivision can be easily expanded to provide for additional services or functions. For example, acquisitions can be easily divided into whatever subdivisions might be necessary—subject area searching, equipment purchasing, etc. It needs to be pointed out that there must be a great deal of cooperation between units when like functions are grouped and that certain functions, while they tend to overlap, are in reality only procedural. The purchase of equipment, which should be carried out in acquisitions, will be done with recommendations from production or equipment services where personnel might be more aware of the technical qualities. Likewise, books may be recommended for purchase by any area, but the physical acquisition is made by acquisitions. This should present no serious problem if administered properly.

Reference should be made to computer services, a function sometimes found within the learning resources services unit. The authors have no strong belief that such services must be there, and various patterns of administering computer service units have developed on different campuses. Regardless of placement, though, a close relationship certainly must be developed with computer services since the computer is of such great service to learning resources functions. If the campus administrative structure dictates that computer services be placed in learning resources, it is suggested that a separate division with a staff relationship to resources and information and instructional technology be created.

Several other functions are "built into" the organization. All of the various divisions and subdivisions are responsible for working with the user. This should be evident in areas such as reference and production, but it might be easy to overlook the fact that technical services also has that responsibility. Inherent in their service are such tasks as selection, catalog maintenance and interpretation (readers' advisor), etc. Duplication here refers only to the printing and duplication of "in-house" publications.

Since Figure 10 is a hypothetical model, its primary use is as a point of departure for developing an organizational structure that best fits the needs of each institution. The model can, and perhaps should, be revised as the needs of the institution dictate and especially as the services within that institution vary. It will provide, however, as all good administrative organizations should, a line and staff relationship for the solution of problems, the implementation of new and creative ideas, and a feeling of cohesiveness within any unit. Above all, it should provide for effective communications in that it has established well-defined lines. The model also has within it, all the inherent weaknesses usually associated with any organizational structure, and only competent management can compensate for those.

THE LIBRARY COMMITTEE

A discussion of the learning resources organization would not be complete without consideration of the faculty library committee. Such a committee, whether made up of faculty and/or students and administration, should be regarded as *advisory* rather than administrative.

In his 1974 study of library committees, Leland Park provided one of the most comprehensive reviews of the history of library committees, as well as additional research on their role. Among other conclusions, Park found that:

1. The committee was considered a needed committee in nearly every case, regardless of agreement or lack of agreement of the committees' functions.

2. While librarians generally agreed that the liaison/advisory role was the only role in which they wanted the committee involved, there was some indication that the committee was used as needed on a selective basis in administrative or policy areas. Encouragement to act in these areas appeared to be at times when the librarian was either unable to make a decision alone or needed additional support in a decision planned.

3. Generally, librarians and committee members did not understand how to effect successfully the liaison/advisory role for the committee. A significant change in this situation could appreciably change the committee's effectiveness for it would include more constituents of the campus as well as assure a regular input of opinions and suggestions to the librarian.

4. The student role on the committee was minimal at best, and nonexistent at worst. There was no uniform commitment to the need for such representation.[5]

The authors believe that the library or learning resources committee can serve a vital advisory role in policy determinations and administrative matters. It can serve as a communications channel and thus help prevent misunderstandings, and it can provide needed support for various budget considerations. In effect, a committee of this sort can provide an added degree of responsiveness in the LRC to the various clientele that it serves, thus adding much-needed credibility to all of its services.

SUMMARY

The organizational structure of the academic library has always been as varied as the role defined for the individual college community itself. Lyle has pointed out that the diversity of the college's mission has resulted in different role definitions for the library too, for "a philosophy of librarianship is hampered by the absence of any national identity of purpose in the college itself and by the fact that one must use the plural form, for college library activities are not confined to anything which may be described as a single pattern."[6] So it is with the learning resource center, for the organizational structure should be directly related to the aims and objectives of the particular institution.

A case in point is the division often labelled public services. Traditionally, it has been and remains a limiting term rather than one that encompasses all public services in the generic sense. In the generic sense, public services becomes the *raison d'être* for the library, for in that sense, all other units of organization—management, technical services, etc.—ought to be subservient to it as an administrative unit. Not only in this sense is the term a misnomer today, though, but it also is in view of expanded services offered by the library or the resource center.

Jerrold Orne has placed this change in perspective in his "Future Academic Library Administration," in *The Academic Library* (1974). Not only does he clearly define the change in scope but also the nature of that change. He stated:

> Public services, as a generic term for all the kinds of services commonly offered by libraries, now suffers from variable acceptance of both words, *public* and *services.* The academic library's publics are now much more numerous than heretofore, and what is perceived as services now includes many more than in earlier times. Traditionally, the academic library served students and faculty of its own institution. Today, there is far greater community involvement, inter-institutional exchange of services, and even national commitments. The very nature of traditional library services, using basically books and journals, is now enlarged to include massive new data banks of useful information, a varied range of new photo-technology products, and other audiovisual representations of information.[7]

As a final word on organizational structure, the authors would like to reinforce the idea that structure ought to be dictated by function. While many aspects of the enlarged scope and workable changes incorporated into learning resources services can remain a part of what has become accepted terminology, it is imperative that by the very magnitude of its services, some form of division based on *function* instead of traditional terminology ought to be conceived. The next four chapters deal with functions of the LRC, but these in themselves should not be necessarily construed as organizational divisions. It is with these functions in mind, however—whether collective, independent, or fragmented—that the organizational structure should be designed. The functional areas the authors have chosen to use are resources and information, instructional technology services, instructional and faculty development, and technical services.

NOTES

[1] Gary T. Peterson, *The Learning Center: A Sphere for Nontraditional Approaches to Education* (Hamden, CT: Linnet, 1975), pp. 22-23.

[2] Arthur M. McAnnally and Robert B. Downs, "The Changing Role of Directors of University Libraries," *College and Research Libraries* 34 (March 1973): 103-125.

[3] Association of College and Research Libraries, *Standards for College Libraries* (Chicago: the author, 1975), p. 10.

[4] G. Edward Evans, *Management Techniques for Librarians* (New York: Academic Press, 1976), pp. 129-30.

[5] Leland M. Park, "The Faculty Library Committee of Six Public Community Colleges in the State of Florida: A Comparative Study Based on Age and Size of the Institution" (Ph.D. dissertation, Florida State University, 1974), pp. 251-54.

[6] Guy R. Lyle, *The Administration of the College Library*, 4th ed. (New York: H. W. Wilson, 1974), pp. 8-9.

[7] Jerrold Orne, "Future Academic Library Administration—Whither or Whether," in *The Academic Library: Essays in Honor of Guy R. Lyle*, ed. Evan Farber and Ruth Walling (Metuchen, NJ: Scarecrow, 1974), pp. 91-92.

RESOURCES AND INFORMATION

If the learning resource center or library is the heart of the academic community, then resources and information are its life blood. The latter terms, though, may have connotations to the print-oriented librarian of public services, and for this reason, the preceding chapter provided a generic definition of public services that greatly expanded the functions commonly associated with this phase of library work. If use of the term persists with its limiting connotation rather than in the generic sense, then perhaps Robert Taylor was correct in his assessment that library service is simply "a reflection of the warehouse syndrome applied by faculty and administration and accepted by librarians."[1] A closer look at the impact the college library's purposes have and should have on the academic community may provide better insight into what the functions of resources and information should be.

Most works on the academic library place some emphasis on its role, and these role definitions reflect the activities generally ascribed to resources and information. It should come as no surprise that library scholars, especially those who work in administration, see these roles as similar in nature, different in scope, but always developed within the framework of the institution's major purposes. It is important to note, too, that many refer to the *educational* role that the LRC so clearly adopts as its central purpose.

James Thompson, in *An Introduction to University Library Administration* (which was directed to British colleges and universities but applies here), did a succinct analysis of the purposes and functions of the college library, all of which can easily be reduced from the broad context to that of resources and information. If one thread ran through his many references to library purpose and function, it was perhaps epitomized in the quotation that Thompson attributed to M. A. Gelfand: "The fundamental role of the library is educational. It should not be operated as a mere storehouse of books attached to a reading-room, but as a dynamic instrument of education."[2]

Among the many who have quoted other leaders or who have espoused theories of their own on how resources have relevance to the clientele in today's academic world, perhaps no one has been quoted himself more often than Robert Taylor. In his book *The Making of a Library: The Academic Library in Transition*, he stated:

Resources are not just rows of books, drawers full of art slides, or shelves of records. Resources are also the conscious exploitation of

these inanimate things to challenge, to suggest, to explicate, to guide—
in short, to educate. This is what libraries are all about.[3]

Even more to the point as to the direction in which the academic library ought to
be moving was Taylor's essay "Patterns Toward a User-Centered Academic Library,"
where he described not only the two scenarios now in existence, but a third that
reflected where libraries ought to be. He outlined this as a situation in which:

> ... the user becomes the center of the institution—not the packages,
> not the systems, but the individuals in the community that is served.
> In this case the academic library will become a true switching center . . .
> in which the process of negotiating and connecting users to people,
> materials, and media is the heart of the enterprise. This may happen
> both inside and outside the building called a "library." It will become a
> "library without walls."[4]

All of this seems to indicate that change in function, scope, and clientele is
coming about. Yet, just as in years past, and without detracting from other aspects
of library administration, it is perhaps public services (in the broadest sense) that
has prompted Lyle and others in works from the 1940s through the 1970s to describe
the library as the indispensible heart of a center of *learning*.

Let it suffice that, for definitive purposes, resources and information will pertain to those activities whereby materials and equipment enable the resource center
to carry out its five generally accepted goals and functions: curriculum support;
independent learning; faculty research; administrative support; and leisure reading,
listening, and viewing. Under no circumstances, however, must these functions be
separated from the functions of such other areas as instructional development and
materials production. All LRCs and libraries would do well to heed Taylor's words
when he decries the grocery store syndrome and encourages libraries "to reduce
repetitive housekeeping functions." He continues:

> This assumes that the librarians really want to rid themselves of
> tedious routines and truly desire time for more critical activities—
> experimenting in the improvement of services, teaching and maybe even
> learning, developing media beyond the book, improving the art of com-
> munication, and developing a sense of community—*because this is what
> libraries are all about.*
> The concept of communicating, the transfer of knowledge, is in
> the best tradition of librarianship, the humanistic tradition, to which
> we pay lip service but little else. If the medium is the message, as the
> prophet says, then the library might be looked on as the totality of all
> media and communication.[5]

This carries implications for the mission of the entire LRC, but it has perhaps
its greatest impact where the functions of resources and information are carried
out. This area has borne the brunt of the warehouse syndrome, and it is this area
that must direct its attention to meeting user needs and to educating them to the
capabilities of resources and information in the life-long learning process. For this
reason, the authors have directed their attention in this chapter to the relationship

of resources and information to the user. The following three areas are explored in the context of the LRC and the user: user resources, user accessibility and education, and user environment.

USER RESOURCES

If LRC personnel are to meet user demands in carrying out the five goals and functions of the resource center (referred to previously), then they must assume that the resources and information collections will have some effect on the range of ideas to which the user will be exposed. While it is certainly imperative to provide a wide range of materials of varying formats (for an idea's validity transcends the mode used for its expression), it is extremely important to establish a program whereby the resource center not only supplies information but also educates the user in the methodology of retrieving it. Nevertheless, it is difficult to do so unless that broad base of ideas in alternative formats exists; consequently, the LRC needs to address itself first of all to the development of that base of ideas.

Collection Development

How then does the LRC differ from the traditional library in collection development? Perhaps not extensively if the traditional library has taken measures to expand its collections beyond materials that have too often been suspect in the academic world and that some librarians have avoided almost to the degree of paranoia. Perhaps the insecurity of working with unfamiliar materials is the predominating factor, and what has developed is a feeling best expressed by Franklin D. Roosevelt, that the thing we need to fear most is fear itself. Then, too, change is always a gradual process, and it is likely that too many librarians suffer from the feelings expressed in George Bernard Shaw's quote from *Major Barbara*: "At first when we learn something new, it feels as if we've lost something."

It would be unfair at this point to leave the impression that the authors subscribe to the theory that the academic library has not changed or expanded its range of materials at all. Rogers and Weber made this point quite clearly when they said:

> It is common practice to use the term *books* generically to cover the vast array of things that make up a research [or academic] library's collections: monographs, serials, phonorecords, films, manuscripts, microtexts, magnetic tapes, broadsides, photographs, prints, video tapes, etc. These graphic media are all in some way distinctively intellectual and informational.[6]

The development of an alternative base of ideas is not a haphazard process, dictated by the whims or idiosyncrasies of those involved in acquisitions. Not only who uses the resources, but also how they are to be used in the learning process become the dominant factors. Charles Churchwell, in placing the purposes of the academic library into focus, sets a standard that would be difficult to dispute for the development of a resource collection. In his article "The Library in Academia: An Associate Provost's View," he made the following statement with respect to purpose: "the library is not free to set its own goals and immediate objectives; it must wait for the colleges and universities it serves to establish their goals, objectives, and educational policies."[7]

It is difficult to fathom an educational policy that does not take into consideration alternative learning formats; translated into a learning resource concept, this implies that selection is a systematic process, based on the needs of users—students, faculty, administrators—and not dictated by a preference for certain formats by those in charge of acquisitions. There are exceptions to such a general rule of selection since funding and facilities can be determining factors; on the other hand, however, these exceptions should not become an excuse for ignoring actual user needs.

Organization of the selection procedure itself will be dealt with in a subsequent chapter on technical processes, for that service function enables the LRC to develop a collection consistent with a selection policy that has as its heart a philosophy derived from the mission statement of the center and an orientation to user needs. Once that has been established, a needs analysis will determine the types of collections most feasible for the academic community that the particular center is to serve. In an essay entitled "Alternative Ways to Meet User Needs," R. Dean Galloway and Zoia Horn made what appears to be an accurate assessment of the role that libraries must play in the development of a base of ideas and in discovering student needs. They stated:

> The techniques of discovering user needs in academic libraries are not highly developed, nor are they often used. The attitude of most academic librarians on this matter is that those needs are already known or, worse yet, that the librarians know what the users *ought* to need. Services are provided for needs that are seldom examined in any systematic or rigorous way.[8]

Certainly if user needs are not considered then accessibility is a minor problem—the resources probably aren't in the collection anyway!

Collection Organization

As a point of departure in speaking of collection building, it should be safe to assume that the LRC, just as the traditional library, will have the three basic collections—circulation, reference, periodicals. Likewise, it will have some or all of the special collections found in various sized libraries—archives, rare books, documents, manuscripts, local history, curriculum, etc. Still other collections may be built around famous writers, historical or literary periods, regional interests, foreign materials, or any such theme as the center may deem appropriate.

In the LRC, alternative materials and related equipment will be incorporated into the collection of materials for the user, either as a separate collection or by being integrated into existing collections. More attention will be given to the organization of nonprint items in a subsequent section on user accessibility; but from the view of collection development and organization, the mere presence of nonprint materials with varying sizes and formats *may* affect the organizational pattern of collections. Some other factors—type of academic institution, its physical size, its enrollment, its traditions, the physical size of the center, budget, personnel—have been and will continue to be factors that influence the organization of resource materials.

Some of these factors, then, are not at all unique to the LRC, for the library has been faced with them for years. Nevertheless, the fact that the LRC makes a deliberate effort to include all alternative formats in building a base of ideas at least intensifies the need for some restructuring within an individual collection or among the collections that constitute the holdings of the center. The name, by the inclusion of the words learning resources, implies that its primary goal is learning. It is unfortunate, but perhaps true, that the technical processing problems of various formats are often the reason such materials are sometimes denied the user by exclusion from the collection.[9]

The merits of inclusion or exclusion of particular learning materials will not be discussed exhaustively, for the acceptance of the learning resources concept in and of itself demands inclusion of all formats. Likewise, the very inclusion of different formats becomes yet another factor, along with those that have always been present, in affecting collection development and organization. While it might be expedient and even welcome, definitive answers cannot be given without examining in detail how fiscal, physical, and human resources can be best applied to serve user needs. Many libraries have worked within the traditional structure and incorporated all formats, or at least some, into their collections, and on other campuses, collections of learning materials, even though separated from the library itself, have been made readily available to users. Neither concept has, however, been universally accepted by all academic librarians.

Passive acceptance of various formats in the academic library can hardly be termed a user-oriented approach to providing an alternative base of ideas for the clientele in the academic community. It appears that many materials have not yet earned the respect of being included in Taylor's "warehouse syndrome," which exists on all too many campuses today; in addition, the organizational conflict that this problem evokes was not even mentioned in a recent article in *College and Research Libraries* dealing with the history of organizational patterns in academic libraries.[10]

For collection development, the implication here ought to be clear: there is more to the learning resources concept than consolidating all materials without any rationale. Simply to close one's eyes to the problems associated with nonprint materials will not make the problem go away, and not to take any action does precious little for the user in the academic community. The first step, it seems, is to accept all formats as useful in learning. No longer can librarians accept the narrow concept of the library and "acceptable" formats for its materials given expression by Bisticci (quoted earlier), who favored only handwritten materials. It is a mind set also suggested in the desk sign that states, "It was all so different before everything changed." And that mind set is not confined to the opinion of the librarian alone, for the authors strongly suspect that they have not been alone in encountering the irate faculty member who decries the addition of microfilm as the most "anti intellectual" and "technologically debasing" thing that could have come into the academic library.

Reference has been made previously to the fact that the learning resource collection does not differ significantly from many library collections except perhaps in scope, and many libraries have espoused the concept of the generic book as promulgated by Shores and by Rogers and Weber. Basically, collections of materials expanded by the addition of alternative learning formats can be developed in much the same way as the library has always encouraged the development and organization of a materials collection. For this reason, the nature of the collection has been emphasized here rather than the method of building collections or of organizing them (i.e., circulation, reference, periodicals, etc.). Almost all library administration books devote some attention to collection organization and development, and the newer books have all been expanded to include the methodology of development. Collection organization theory in most of those books remains traditional, but these books can nevertheless serve as models. The titles of these books are listed both in the notes and the "Additional References" section.

Human Resources

There is, however, one resource that is too often excluded from the academic library but that should be included for its clientele: the vast array of human and physical resources available both within and outside the academic community. Certainly these resources, whether through addition to the collection by way of audio and video tape, film, slide-sound, etc., or simply through bibliographic reference in the card catalog, should be made available as potential sources of information for the LRC user. Field trips and human resources not only could be located through the center but also scheduled by staff with expertise in this realm. These resources, along with inter-library loans, cooperative services, and networking, can increase user resources in quantity and in quality. In effect, local and oral history programs do this for history and related fields, and it certainly is not too unrealistic to expect that similar effort could be expended in other areas of the humanities and sciences, in industry and technology, in business and economics, and in almost any academic endeavor.

It may seem to the reader that an entirely too conservative, traditional approach to user resources has been taken by the authors. This stems partially from the fact that the traditional organizational structure can lend itself to the development of a materials collection in the LRC. However, we must not overlook the fact that accessibility to the collection is the link between the user and the resources, and that will, in the final analysis, determine the organizational pattern. Connie Dunlap, whose recent article was cited previously, highlighted Doralyn Hickey's observation that:

> ... library services are designed to move materials through the system and on to storage shelves, there to be interpreted by a group of people who have had little or nothing to do with the procedures which put the material into storage. She suggests that a fairly obvious solution to such a dilemma is to reorient the library systems around the concept of direct and effective service and the clientele. What currently exists is an orientation toward indirect service; and if any direct service is involved, it is aimed at the preservation and storage of materials rather than the solution of users' problems. Thus, the library might consider whether its service should become client centered rather than material

centered. If librarians take too seriously the responsibility to focus upon users' needs, they might be forced to a totally different pattern of work organization.[11]

Reference here is obviously to collection organization as it affects public (in the traditional sense) and technical services, but the principle exactly expresses the user dilemma. It is quite possible that the LRC director needs to take a hard and challenging look at how to organize resources and information collections, especially in relation to user accessibility. In the final analysis, accessibility plays the major role in how the collection of resources is organized.

USER ACCESSIBILITY AND EDUCATION

A collection of books does not make a library, nor does an expanded base of alternative formats make an LRC. Kevin Guinagh stated this fact quite accurately when he said:

> The vitality of the modern college depends to a great extent on the resources of its library; however, it is hardly necessary to point out that a collection may be ever so rich but if it is not used, its wealth is purely ornamental. Such libraries may be compared to collections of Aldines or incunabula whose owners are unable to read the volumes they treasure.[12]

Likewise, learning resources, with respect to resources and information, becomes a vital, integral part of the academic learning environment only when it brings users and the material they actually need together. Accessibility means an ultimate joining of user and idea in whatever format that idea is expressed. Equally important (beginning perhaps at just that moment, and certainly extending over a period of time) is the development of those skills that enable the user, through bibliographic search and physical retrieval, to become independent and competent in the quest for resources and information. This is not only vital if the academic community is to be served effectively and the five-fold functions of the resource center are to be met, but also if the user is to be expected to become a life-long user of resources and information through post-college learning.

Direct and Indirect Service

Allowing accessibility through the provision of good bibliographic control of resources and information is not new, and most works on reference services make mention of the American Library Association's "Reference Standards," which place reference and information services in two classes—direct and indirect.[13] More often than not these services are provided on a need basis by either readers' services or reference services, both divisions or functions of the traditional library. William Katz placed the indirect service in focus when he stated:

More specifically, not only does indirect reference service consist of compiling bibliographies but it has to do with selection and organization of materials, the evaluation of the service and the collections, interlibrary loan, and a number of "housekeeping" chores from filing to photocopying.[14]

Direct reference service, according to the "Reference Standards," comes in a variety of ways, of which the most common are information service and instruction, and it consists "of personal assistance provided to library patrons in pursuit of information."[15]

Accessibility

Resource and information retrieval is built around accessibility, and accessibility is central to each of the five functions referred to previously. Accessibility, in turn, rests not on only bibliographic accessibility, but also on physical accessibility, both of which put resources and information within reach of the user. It is essential that efforts be concentrated on providing a functional catalog (or its equivalent), good reference service, and easy physical access to all formats of materials, regardless of handling or location. When these are viewed from the user assistance aspect, competency development in searching, selecting, and retrieval become paramount. A breakdown in any one of these aspects in the process of bringing user and information together is likely to turn away a potential user-learner and to kill any enthusiasm generated at that particular time for the use of resources. More unfortunately, however, it may have turned the user away from establishing the habit of becoming a life-long LRC user, a tragic milestone for future educational endeavors of that client.

With this prospect in mind, the LRC must subscribe fully to the concept of direct and indirect reference services. The entire use of the information and resources collection must be built around accessibility and instruction for the user, whether seeking a resource or information, using the card catalog or an index, or receiving instruction through orientation, a curriculum-related instructional program, or on a one-to-one basis.

A Functional Catalog

Although many institutions are turning away from the traditional card catalog as the means of bibliographic accessibility, in most academic settings, it still functions, along with indexes and bibliographies, as the primary accessibility tool for the user. In reporting that many major libraries have closed, or plan to close, their library catalogs, J. McRee Elrod stated:

> The fact that these major libraries are seeking alternatives to the card catalogue should cause us to pause and look again at the problem of this form of the catalogue which has held almost unquestioned sway in North American libraries for generations of librarians.[16]

It is unfortunate that all too often the decision to do something about the card catalog comes about both because of technical difficulties for those that create the catalog and because of the librarian's inability to teach the user to master the complexities of such bibliographic access. There appear to be two avenues open to the media center in its approach to make the catalog, in whatever form, more serviceable and practicable for the user: to reduce its complexity and to provide instruction in its use (either on an individual basis or as part of the educational program of the college). Hopefully, both will be used.

Elrod suggested some good changes, but he emphasized that change begins with decreasing the reluctance to change.[17] Charles McClure proposed a drastic revision in the subject approach, and his study of subject and added entries as access points to information led him to make the following statements in his discussion:

> For the patron who is attempting to obtain subject access to library information via the card catalog, this study provides little to be optimistic about.... One might question seriously the use of the card catalog as a subject access point to information.
> ... Perhaps we should discontinue subject added entries and replace them with machine produced subject catalogs where the *work* will be subject indexed and *not* the book.... And librarians could stop making excuses for the rather poor performance of the card catalog as a tool for subject access to information.[18]

This can be summarized as a caution that the new technologies do not necessarily provide all the answers and that awaiting solutions through technology should not diminish our attempts to improve what we presently have.

The key to most resource and information collections is still a functional catalog, and the functional catalog, along with indexes and bibliographies, provides the user with bibliographic access. It matters little whether the access comes in traditional forms (i.e., card catalog, book catalog, divided catalog, periodical indexes, reference bibliographies, etc.); whether it is produced on cards, computer print-outs, microforms, magnetic tape, or some other method yet to be devised; or where the bibliographic data base is generated (i.e., produced locally, purchased from some source, or acquired through networking). What matters is that a functional bibliographic access system, whether in a card catalog form or not, be reduced to its least complex nature for the sake of the user. It must provide access to the widest possible range of resources and information in all formats in such a manner that it becomes usable, and the user must be encouraged, aided, and abetted to become a competent user of the bibliographic data base. Attention thus must be directed toward user education in all aspects of library service, keeping in mind that the resource center must assume a responsibility for and an acceptance of change in making the card catalog functional from the user's point of view.

User Instruction

In order for the learning resource client to use the resources and information available, an orientation to and an understanding of the card catalog must be provided. This presents the media center staff with its first educational objective, one that is all too often passed over as something that the user already knows. Joan Marshall has placed the user's inability to use the card catalog in perspective when she stated:

> The catalog access we provide to materials, however they may be housed, is a separate and far more serious problem [than the organization of materials which leaves something to be desired]. Some aspects of it vary from library to library. . . . Other aspects of the problem, however, plague all of us equally. . . .
>
> One . . . arises from our refusal to recognize that the card catalog, since it imposes order, is inevitably complex. Academic librarians, particularly, have ducked the service implications of this fact by hiding behind the assumption that their users are either scholars accustomed to bibliographic conundrums or potential scholars who should be trained—i.e., should be left to flounder for themselves—in the use of the card catalog.[19]

If one accepts Marshall's statement, and the authors believe she is correct, and if one endorses the thesis espoused by Rogers and Weber that "the most significant step the library can take in fostering general education is to provide freedom of access to collections," then professional help must be provided in some manner to help the user understand and utilize the catalog.[20]

The same is, of course, true of bibliographies found in the reference collection and of indexes provided for the use of specific reference services and periodicals. Some of these are difficult enough for skilled librarians to interpret and use, so it is essential that the student or faculty member be provided the help and instruction necessary to use them competently and independently. The card catalog, bibliographies, indexes, and access to outside sources of information are essential ingredients of user accessibility and, as such, must become a part of any type of user education program.

In the opinion column in the *Journal of Academic Librarianship*, Joe Boisse expressed his opinion on library instruction, which characterizes quite accurately the status of library instruction today:

> While bibliographic instruction is not an entirely new concept, for the most part librarians have historically relied on accidental contact between students and themselves. In so doing, we have managed to reach only a minuscule number of students. As a result, the great majority of undergraduates have received a degree without ever acquiring basic research skills which would be useful to them both professionally and personally.[21]

Interesting enough, he did not even include the importance of library instruction for the student in fulfilling the requirements of academic work, but then that implication may well have been there. Boisse's opinion is shared by many librarians and supported in a multitude of studies.[22] Betty Young, in her work on circulation service, cited some of the major studies on circulation work, use studies, and user attitudes, and they can perhaps be best summarized in the words of Robert Taylor, whom she quoted:

Libraries are very frustrating systems to use. . . . Catalogs, indexes, classification schemes . . . are intended to help the user. For the naive user, however, they are terribly sophisticated and much too intricate . . . awkward in fact. They have been designed by librarians for librarians.[23]

Young's appraisal that, "in recent thought, then, instruction in library use appears to be closely tied to service, and the level of user satisfaction is related to the assistance given at the time of need" is rather apropos.[24]

The place to establish a good program of library instruction appears to be the undergraduate level, regardless of the size of the institution, regardless of the nature of the students, and regardless of faculty opposition to it. Allan Dyson, in a study on the organization of undergraduate library instruction, laid the groundwork for development of such a program. He set both the pattern and the objective when he stated in his conclusions:

Each of these patterns evolves as a reflection of local conditions, and it is impossible to say that all libraries should organize their instruction in one particular way. . . .

A basic objective of academic librarianship must be that every student, by the time that he or she completes an undergraduate education should be able to make effective use of library resources. To strive for less is to deny our professional responsibilities.[25]

Another interesting study that sets forth some solid research data for initiation of a good library instruction program was conducted at Sangamon State University (Springfield, Illinois). Implications of the program at Sangamon were adequately described by Howard Dillon, University Librarian, when he stated:

Although the organization described has been developed under special circumstances surrounding the creation of a new university, its philosophical and theoretical roots are implanted in a rich literature concerning the role of the academic librarian. It is hoped that this example will encourage others to experiment with new models and new roles for staff that will enable their libraries to become stronger as "teaching libraries."[26]

In light of the Sangamon success, it would be well for the LRC in an institution of any size to become acquainted with both Dillon's premises concerning library learning and the competencies set forth as the primary goal of library instruction. Those premises were:

1. That library resources are a vital component in the educational process and, as such, adequate collections are necessary as curricular programs are initiated;
2. That library resources should reflect a multi-media approach to learning and, therefore, include both print and non-print materials; and

3.   That library competence is a valid objective of liberal education and, as such, the library has a responsibility to teach this competence.

The competencies for the primary instructional goal, suitable for a LRC were:

1.   Knowledge of the basic kinds of print and non-print materials available and how they are arranged;
2.   Knowledge of basic bibliographic tools and how to use them.
3.   Knowledge of specific bibliographic tools in a particular area of interest and how to use them;
4.   Knowledge of other subject areas related to the primary area of interest and how to find reference to them; and
5.   Ability to define a problem or an aspect of a problem within a particular area of interest and to limit and select materials most relevant to it.[27]

The authors of this work suggest the addition of at least one competency: ability to use equipment associated with the use of basic kinds of nonprint materials.

The articles by Dyson and Dillon can provide the learning resource director with the framework in which a good library education program can be established, and additional programs are based on the general conclusions suggested by Dyson (involve large number of library staff; provide alternatives in learning; gain commitment by library administration; and accept that all students need it). It then becomes within the realm of possibility to overcome what Evan Farber calls the "university-library syndrome."[28] He stated:

The faculty member's academic background and training work against an understanding of the proper role of the college library. He has been trained as a scholar-researcher and is not really interested in *how* his students use the library; he, after all, learned to use it in his discipline and he assumes students can also. Moreover, if students need help, they can either come to him and he'll recommend titles they should use, or they can of course ask the reference librarian. Rarely does it occur to him that learning *how* to use the library intelligently and independently is not only a desirable part of the educational process but will also permit students to do better work for him, and certainly the idea that anyone else can lead his students through the intricacies of his discipline's material is foreign to him.[29]

Inherent in this syndrome also is the fact that the faculty member is all too often not aware of the expanding nature of the resources center. Certainly, the faculty member, too, must become a part of the library education program if the faculty is to foster the use of all resources by students. A faculty orientation to the LRC and its philosophy of expanded collections and services, expressed either independently or collectively through faculty groups, is essential. The reader can look to LOEX (Library Orientation Exchange, centered at Eastern Michigan University) for assistance in establishing library instruction programs, but every program should involve both the director and all the staff members. However, with respect to resources and information, the brunt of the instruction will fall to reference services. Faculty education in the realm of instructional technology and production services will fall to that division. One of the better works dealing with library instruction is the chapter by Nancy Hammond in Cowley's work.[30]

Summarizing the whole aspect of user education, the learning resource center must assume as its role a responsibility to educate, but not just to show the methodology of the card catalog. It must provide information also as to the use of each unique collection (with its own particular indexes), give users opportunities to acquire some dexterity and familiarity with the equipment necessary to use resources, and demonstrate for users the intricacies of resource and information retrieval wherever these are located. It must also be directed toward all users on a need basis in whatever manner is most suitable.

Physical Accessibility

Along with bibliographic accessibility comes the second side of accessibility; namely, the user must be able to retrieve either the physical item desired and/or the information needed from it. It does little for users if they possess the bibliographic ability to locate the resources or information, but are still unable to get access to it. Nor does it help them if the librarian provides the help needed to locate information and resources but then is unable to produce the physical item or the information because of some difficulty in the retrieval methodology. Factors that the learning resource center needs to consider with respect to physical accessibility are: centralization versus decentralization; closed versus open shelving; integrated shelving; integrated versus separate collections; circulation policies; and location of equipment.

Centralization Versus Decentralization

The problems associated with decentralization of resource collections are not new, and these collections bring up the problem of accessibility, which has been magnified for the LRC because of its rapid growth. Prior to institutional collections of nonprint materials (either separate from or within the library), many departmental collections existed as "teaching materials." In the traditional sense, many of these were based on printed works that developed into departmental or school/college libraries. Often they were not well organized, grew like Topsy, and were tagged with her same lineage; in many larger institutions, however, these grew and prospered into excellent libraries. Nonprint materials present a different problem since many faculty members still look at these as "teaching materials" only and not as materials that may have interest for other users in independent study or leisure viewing/listening. This attitude has made it difficult to make these materials physically available and accessible to other users, and, as with so many other educational changes, it can take years of persistence or a retirement to bring about even bibliographic control. Problems associated with decentralized collections, ever present and ever expanding, need to be solved if accessibility is to become a reality.

Most of the studies regarding the need to decentralize are quite dated, but nevertheless they present some interesting aspects that might be useful in determining the direction in which the resource center is to proceed. E. W. Erickson, in reporting on a survey covering the years 1938-1952, indicated that 64 out of 146 libraries surveyed reported concern about the ills of decentralization.[31] Dunlap gave perhaps the best report in her 1976 article in *College and Research Libraries* on the history of the problem: "The question of centralization or decentralization and the problems attendant to it have probably created as much controversy as any other organizational problem in libraries."[32] It is also interesting to note, and certainly significant today, to consider the pro and con arguments of Robert Miller's study, as presented by Dunlap. His arguments were placed in seven categories—accessibility, cost, efficiency, adequacy, use, interrelations of subject fields, and educational significance. Only accessibility was considered as a positive factor in decentralization, although an adequate budget, if sufficient to maintain both the central collection and the decentralized collections, could be a factor working in favor of decentralization.[33]

It is unlikely that today's spiraling costs and the increasing proliferation of materials caused by the rapid growth of knowledge will let us duplicate the necessary materials and provide the services needed to expand toward more decentralized collections. Hard and fast answers about departmental collections or college/school libraries that already exist are not easy to provide, but a few general guidelines will give some direction to their development as a vital part of the learning resource collection.

While retrieval and accessibility may remain severe problems, they can and must be reduced considerably if the user is to benefit. All decentralized materials must be cataloged for bibliographic control and accessibility, the centers must be staffed properly by professional and clerical staff members to provide information and retrieval services, proper hours must be established to make materials readily available, and funds must be provided both to develop the center properly and to take care of the need to duplicate materials and services. This may be an expensive manner of handling these materials and services, but if the institution is truly interested in serving the user, then it must provide this kind of support.

Whatever decisions concerning decentralization are reached, it will be well for the resource center to heed the words of Robert Taylor: "If the user cannot obtain something the catalog informs him the Library has, easily and without excessive bureaucracy and dispersion, then the Library has failed in one of its major public interfaces." Taylor then pointed out the study by Victor Rosenberg wherein he indicated "that 'ease of access' to an information system is more significant than 'amount or quality' of information obtained."[34] This has implications in that, if bibliographic access is provided to a decentralized collection, then delivery of resources must be both quick and effective with a minimum of hassle for the user.

Integrated Versus Separate Collections

Another of the immediate problems facing the LRC is whether its format dictates the establishment of a special collection or whether all materials should be integrated into existing collections. In either case, an integrated catalog should exist. The problem of integrating collections is not as simple as it appears on the surface, though, for combinations of the two extremes exist. Some formats (e.g., microforms) already often exist as separate collections within collections, while still other formats (e.g., documents) are sometimes made part of several collections.

It would appear that the LRC is presented with three viable alternatives in the handling of various learning formats: 1) establishment of a completely separate collection of those materials not found in traditional collections; 2) partial integration of any materials easily assimilated into existing collections; and 3) complete integration of all formats into existing collections. In looking at integration versus separation from the user point of view, it is apparent that the last alternative is perhaps the most desirable, but closer analysis of each does present some problems.

Arguments against integration of all learning materials into the other collections are those of easy pilferage, destruction, difficulty of handling odd formats, and easy misshelving. Perhaps the most susceptible to being stolen is the audio cassette, even though it can be altered so that it can be used as a playback tape only. This in itself may not deter the user from stealing it, but the detect system and special display racks present solutions to that problem. While it may be true that a user can mutilate a costly film, the same can be said of a costly set of books. A misshelved item is the same as a lost item if it cannot be located when needed, but that problem is one to which the library still seeks a solution even with print materials. Perhaps it is only when LRC personnel become a bit more trustful of its clients that some sense of responsibility can be developed in them. That may indeed have a theoretical ring to it, but it has already been substantiated in studies, as noted in Taylor,[35] that there is indeed a correlation between accessibility and use.

Integrated Shelving

How materials are shelved within collections may also affect the accessibility to them. Certainly, from the user standpoint, complete integration is the preferable way to shelve. Institutions such as the College of Dupage in Illinois and the University of Wisconsin—Stout have done so successfully on a limited basis, but any measure of success must still withstand the test of time. Inconsistency of format presents some major problems for intershelving of materials, as does the fact that some small items (either individually or as parts of a kit) are subject to easy pilferage or loss. Electronic detect systems may be the answer for pilferage, but the answer for intershelving is not quite as simple. It is not impossible, however, since several options are open (and other avenues may need to be developed). One option is to develop packages for each item or to substitute decoy blocks with retrieval numbers, but either of these is costly in time, money, and space.

A compromise solution might be to group materials in already available packages of approximately book size (i.e., filmstrip packages that hold nine or twelve strips in one book-size package). These can then be conveniently placed into the regular collection within specialized divisions or subdivisions of the classification system in use. An example would be to place filmstrips on American history, classified in the 970s, at the head of the 970 Dewey section; the same could be done with other formats. In one respect, many institutions now do this with their microform collections. In this manner, nonprint items would be handled like all printed works as to location—general circulation, reserve, reference, periodicals, etc.

It is apparent that the merits of integrated shelving are open to debate since not enough institutions have tried, analyzed, and reported the results of such experiments. A factor that must be given consideration is that each institution must analyze its own particular needs and make a determination based on them. In the final analysis, what is good for one academic community may not be at all good for another; but certainly if no one does experimental work in these areas, change is unlikely to occur.

Closed Versus Open Shelves

The concept of closed shelves has disappeared from most small and medium-sized academic libraries except for certain collections (i.e., reserve, periodicals, nonprint); but there is a great deal of speculation that, with the continued growth of knowledge and a leveling off in building programs, it may return again in the not too distant future. If the concept of zero growth espoused by Daniel Gore becomes a reality, then many materials may go into closed shelves since these would not be available to the local patron except by request.[36] (The authors are aware that the term zero growth may be a misnomer.) Despite some very rational objections to it by knowledgeable people in the academic library field, it still may have some implications for the future. Both the closed shelf concept and zero growth should be watched closely for implications they may have for the user.

Except for special collections, many libraries have opened their stacks in most areas to all users, and certainly for graduate students and faculty members. What should or should not be placed on closed shelves is not easily determined, and each institution must make its own decisions based on an analysis of user demands. If one factor should be taken into consideration in setting policies regarding open versus closed shelving, it was well defined by Taylor when he cited Rosenberg's study wherein ease of access was more significant than the amount or quality, and which he supported by stating that the center should provide easy access without excessive bureaucracy.[37] A few comments about certain collections might help to provide some guidelines in policy making.

Closed Collections

One collection most commonly placed in closed stacks has been the reserve collection. Studies have shown that these collections are not generally well used and that to place materials in closed stacks for a few is to deprive many others of access to them. One solution appears to be to let faculty members who are serious about reserve books make their own arrangements to have them placed there, and, at the time they do this, to encourage them to place those books on limited circulation (i.e., overnight, three day, five day, etc.) but left on the open shelves. Faculty members will generally be receptive to this type of arrangement if they can be convinced that their students will in fact have access to the materials. Policy makers in the area of reserve collections should acquaint themselves with the studies conducted at St. Cloud State University (Minnesota) and the universities of Arizona and Nebraska.[38]

Tradition has played a part in prompting many libraries to place nonprint items on closed shelves. One of the most common arguments for this policy is that these items do not lend themselves to browsing as do print materials. This may well be true of some items, but others have information that does lend itself to browsing (i.e., record jackets, study guides, kit materials, etc.). If the items must be used with some type of listening or viewing equipment, then provision should be made for easy access to that type of equipment in the immediate area of the material.

Access to periodicals and microforms has also often been limited to closed shelves because of mutilation, pilferage, and misshelving or misfiling. Answers again are difficult to provide, but some attention must be directed to the fact that if these items are not easily accessible then they will not be used to the fullest; consequently, we must expect some problems. Perhaps these can be reduced through better user education, by asking the user not to reshelve or refile the items, and by circulation of these items even though it might have to be on a limited basis. Some of these problems were discussed in the section on integrated shelving, and development of responsibility and user education still appear to be the best answers.

Circulation and Related Equipment

Closely related to closed shelving is circulation of materials. Policies vary greatly from library to library, and accessibility has not always been a factor that has held much esteem in developing those policies. More often than not, circulation has been a tradition that can be traced back to locked chests and chained books. Galloway and Horn, citing a study at Cal State, spoke succinctly to circulation policies:

> A relaxed attitude toward circulation of materials is essential to providing good service. . . . All materials, except the most rare and special treasures should be circulated if there is a need for it.
> . . . A short term loan period makes no sense for seldom-used items which the user needs for a long time. If the user must return or renew materials in two or three weeks, or perhaps pay an overdue fine, when no one else wants them, the user has been poorly served.[39]

The staid, tradition-bound concepts used to develop circulation policies cannot be fostered if the LRC is to provide the type of accessibility that will encourage use. Better policies will also help libraries to reduce the "warehouse syndrome" referred to previously.

The inclusion of nonprint materials in the collection demands the development of some policy concerning equipment collections. If the user is to have access to the data base of ideas and information that includes audio and video formats, then access to playback equipment is also imperative. (The reference here to equipment concerns only that equipment used in conjunction with the resources and information collections, not equipment used in production or in the classroom.) As a guiding principle, the main access point for equipment used in connection with nonprint materials should be in the area where those materials are distributed.

This would require that all types of equipment required for listening and viewing in a particular area actually be provided for use in that area; any portable equipment that can be easily checked out should also be made accessible at that point. Nonportable types of equipment or the difficult to transport should be checked out from a central distribution point, which in turn should be located in production/instructional technology services, since a central inventory of campus equipment is best kept in this area. The acquisition, maintenance, and control of equipment will be discussed in more detail in the chapter on technical services.

USER ENVIRONMENT

One last aspect of resources and information remains to be discussed: user environment. User and resources are brought physically together in a certain place, which also involves the people who work there. While the authors have previously stated that the key to linking user and resource or idea is accessibility both in the bibliographic and physical sense, environment can also be a factor. Just as user education must be designed to increase accessibility, so too will an effective user environment have an impact on both accessibility and use. The intent in speaking of user environment is to describe a setting that is most conducive to bringing the user to the resources and information so that a life-long habit of using the resource center, and of doing so often, can be fostered. Facilities and personnel could also have been included under accessibility since they affect that part of library service, but its treatment as a separate facet reinforces its importance.

While the environment of the LRC is dictated to a large extent by the nature of its staff, the type of facility, and the amount of fiscal resources available to establish a library program, it is essential that within those limitations, environmental guidelines be based on user demands. An assessment of faculty and student needs and a subsequent evaluation of this data will provide the means for adopting or adapting policies that affect the environment of the center. Some factors, such as the respective sizes of faculty and student body, lend themselves as quantitative data for decision making, but other factors more qualitative in nature must be sought through user input and evaluation.

A well-designed user environment creates an atmosphere that encourages the user, whether faculty or student, to use the facility and to take advantage of the services offered there. The two factors most likely to create that kind of atmosphere are the learning resource staff and the facility itself, both taken in their broadest senses. Superseding the placement of competent personnel in positions that have well-defined job descriptions are personality characteristics that should be considered in employment; and if such considerations are not possible, then they should be considered in the placement of personnel in certain key positions.

Likewise, if a new building is scheduled for construction, it can be planned to make optimum use of space so that the best possible user accessibility to areas, collections, information, and services can be provided. If learning resource services has to adapt to an older building, unique physical factors can be taken into consideration to provide an atmosphere more attractive and conducive to use. Indeed, variables in staff and facilities can be controlled to make the atmosphere of the LRC such that it is attractive to the user.

Personnel

Most works on library administration have a chapter or section devoted to personnel, but few of these transcend academic preparation and a committment to what Lyle has called mental attainment. Additionally, a few references to such factors as employment of persons of integrity and avoidance of employment of persons likely to become personnel problems are also included.[40] Generally, too, most of these works deal with the mechanics of employment and employee management. The authors do not wish to minimize the importance of these factors in personnel management, and a later chapter will deal with some of those very aspects. The aspect to which the authors wish to direct attention here, though, is how the employee performs within the requirements of a specific position and how that performance is likely to affect the user. Is it unreasonable to assume that, if (as pointed out earlier) ease of access to materials is more important than the quality of the resources, then perhaps ease of access to library personnel, either physical access directly or through approachability, is also highly important? Personnel may have to understand that the development of rapport with a user is just as essential in the library as it is in the teaching process; and that there are factors that affect the performance level of individuals in service related positions.

The development of good human relations skills, however that may be accomplished, is essential in personnel development. The many ramifications of relating well with others should stimulate personnel to develop attitudes that will help rather than discourage people from using the resources of the center. Personnel who carry out their duties in a professional manner, displaying a measure of confidence and intellectualism, can only enhance their work with the user by a warm, friendly, sincere attitude reflecting integrity and openness. Set in an atmosphere of impartiality toward both faculty member and student, such a person becomes an accepted member of the academic community and quickly gains the respect of those served. Once an atmosphere of service permeates the entire LRC, then the personnel can go about developing a program of resource development and use that has as its heart those services and instruction that can make the user not only competent but also a repeater.

Paul Wasserman described how personality characteristics can be an impediment for those who propose change, and he reinforces the fact that people do react on the basis of personality characteristics:

> Those who in manner, dress, or attitude create antagonism, as do many who wage war against the status quo, may be rejected without serious attention to the merit of their proposals. For their behavior offends the congenial atmosphere and thereby engenders antipathy. While the individual and not the idea is the offender, both become the targets of those who are offended. . . . Appealing personality is often a more valuable asset than prestige, since it is flexible and can be manipulated with ease. It does not depend upon past accomplishment, is adjustable and dynamic, and can reflect the circumstances of the moment. Its immediacy gives it precedence over estimates made on the basis of other, more rigorous criteria. Its overriding influence is reflected in the way in which such high premium is placed upon personal relations.[41]

Translated into a service-oriented approach toward the user this implies that the staff cannot be tolerant of an attitude that seeks personal freedom at any cost. It is not the intent here to suggest that the LRC must develop a homogeneous staff. A heterogeneous staff will also provide the user with alternatives in seeking help from persons who reflect and more easily accept that user's values.

Yet, while buildings, collections, instructions, and orientation are certainly important, personality characteristics supersede them because in providing service to the user, staff members are involved in a person-to-person relationship. They can ill afford to "turn off" the user by unacceptable personality characteristics and attitudes when it is within their realm to develop dynamic personal and human relations that will foster better use of the resources and services offered by the center.

This concept reflects what constitutes an atmosphere in which academic freedom for all can be attained, and it is not, as might appear at first glance, an impingement on academic freedom. When considering placement of personnel, managers need to remember the difference between personality characteristics, and personal freedoms. Not to provide service to all in the academic community, even through such an indirect way as by discouraging the user through poor human relations and attitudes, reflects a lack of commitment to the educational process within that community.

Service Orientation

In addition to the competency and personality characteristics, the LRC personnel must be service-oriented to provide an environment that will bring the user to the center. This has implications for areas other than resources and information, but certain activities on the part of personnel can help to improve the image of those involved in resources and information as truly being user oriented. Basic to this is the fact that users have a central access point that can be reached either by phone or in person; so information about resources, services, or simply referral to other staff members can be made easily and without hassle. Only the most persistent user will continue to persevere if repeatedly given incorrect information or improper referral at this initial contact.

The conscientious, service-oriented librarian will make certain that within the limits of human possibility any service area will be adequately and properly staffed at all times. This begins with a dedication of personal availability to the user. When that is impossible, make certain that the user is given the proper help either at that moment or upon the return of the person to the service area. It should also mean that the person in any duty area will take the first step and make the little extra effort required to fulfill the user's needs. Perhaps this involves a return call, or a simple message to the user that while the answer to the request is not known, an effort will be made to find one. The user should be notified as quickly as possible. Particularly important in such a situation is an awareness of the options available to help the user—direct referral to the proper person, referral service on a reference question when a reference specialist is not on duty, referral of acquisitions requests to the acquisitions personnel, individual instructional help in any phase of learning resource collection use, bibliographic search, etc.

In the final analysis, the matching of positions to personnel upon some well-conceived plan will result in an effective work atmosphere that is not only good for the employee but also for the patron. A text such as that by G. Edward Evans entitled *Management Techniques for Librarians* can be instrumental in providing the framework wherein personnel management and development become systematic and effective. He placed the relationship of personnel to position in perspective with the following statement:

> Job requirements have several dimensions in addition to the essential skills, knowledge, training, and aptitude. Also required are specific personal and emotional qualities. Any employer prefers hiring a person who is stable, is likely to remain with the organization, who will work and be interested in the work, who can get along with co-workers and the supervisor, and who will have regular attendance and be prompt. Personal appearance and manner of speaking are important in public service positions. Social ability, initiative, and drive are also the essential in any job dealing with the public, such as in the reference department where the individual must be able to approach patrons and make them feel comfortable.[42]

Physical Facilities

While not as major a detriment to user atmosphere as poor personal attitudes and characteristics, the atmosphere provided within a facility in its physical arrangements and environment can also be limiting. Almost any work on library administration includes a section on facility planning, and a literature search will reveal a sufficient amount of material to help plan a proper user environment in a center. Rogers and Weber summarized the generally accepted aspects of facility planning as follows:

> . . . Students and faculty members have heightened expectations with respect to pleasant surroundings, ample light without glare, colors that are pleasing, ventilation that is adequate, temperatures that are comfortable, acoustics that protect the reader from undue distraction, and seating and work surfaces that facilitate long and often intense concentration. An effective working environment for staff and readers can be a vital element in transforming a great collection of books into a great working library.[43]

These same principles can be extended to the LRC (allowing for some different types of activities), especially as they pertain to nonprint materials and such services as instructional technology and production. With respect to general criteria, the LRC should strive to be a warm and open place, physically reflecting comfort and aesthetic quality. But physical attractiveness can mean more than merely aesthetic quality, since much of what is used to produce the effect can come in the way of motivational or directional graphics designed to increase user effectiveness. Such an approach can be yet another way to reach the individual learner in the program of user instruction.

Graphics can take the form of a directory near the main entry to parts of the building, floor plans indicating locations of materials and services on particular floors, collection and service identification, and displays of materials to increase listening, viewing, and reading. This will provide the user with visual aids to seek information or services, but such aids must be of high quality with elements of composition, balance, color, simplicity, readability, and overall appeal.

If at all possible, consideration should be given to the user in establishing the kinds of areas to be made available. These areas must reflect user demands, needs, and learning styles by providing space for independent or small group study, larger reading rooms when desirable, an auditorium or classroom facility for instructional and/or multi-media presentations, and areas for independent listening and viewing. These can be included in planning for a new facility; but even in an old facility, every effort should be made to meet user needs for these types of areas. In planning for user needs in the area of resources and information, especially insofar as user atmosphere is a factor, much information is available.

Hours

An empirical study of any library or LRC will reveal that many of the users are there simply to study, and provisions must be made to accommodate those users. Some libraries have provided twenty-four hour study areas for the user; but, while the number of hours is flexible and should be based on user needs, it is imperative that the academic community provide such a place, preferably in or near the library. An excellent survey regarding student reactions to study facilities was undertaken by a special committee on establishing a new college and presented to the presidents of Amherst, Mount Holyoke, Smith, and Massachusetts.[44] While the information is dated, it does provide a model for research, and other, more recent studies are also available in the literature. The hours of service, however, must be developed around the needs of the clientele, and each LRC should conduct its own study on student needs.

While not directly related to atmosphere, hours do become a factor in user accessibility, and they do affect the environment in which student or faculty member works. Hours are a delicate area in terms of public relations and the final determination of what is to be rests somewhere between twenty-four hours (which is what the students sometimes demand) and more reasonable hours (usually suggested by the staff) so that better service can be offered. Compromises can be made so that service need not suffer and users need not be antagonized, but such actions need to be made on the basis of sound judgment, operational costs, and user patterns. As a rule of thumb, when students demand longer hours, it is usually because they need a quiet place to study; library materials and services are not necessarily involved. There are at least three factors that should be considered in determining hours: the provision of a study facility to take care of that aspect of user needs; extension of library hours but reduction of professional staff time by providing referral services in areas when need for professional help may arise; and extension of library hours during peak usage times (e.g., first week of term, midterm, final weeks of the term, etc.).

The LRC functions within certain limitations as to budget, staff, and facility, but an analysis of all of these in relation to user needs will help to determine the type of atmosphere that needs to be created. In summary, the atmosphere and the environment in which the user wants to work do affect the amount of use that can be expected, as do procedures and policies that reflect the best thinking in placement of personnel and in development of facilities.

SUMMARY

Systematic planning in the development of resource and information collections and services underlies good service to the academic community. Policies and procedures must be developed on the basis of user needs and patterns, but these must be periodically evaluated. To provide a sound base of alternative ideas, the LRC must provide materials in all types of formats, make them accessible both bibliographically and physically, and provide an environment in which optimum use can be made of collections and services. A well-defined program of instruction, systematically planned for implementation on both an individual basis and on a curriculum-related group basis, is essential in meeting the purposes of the resource center to develop competent, life-long users of the collections and services. Optimum use can be fostered only if intelligent decisions regarding collection development, placement, user accessibility, and user environment are made on the basis of data analysis concerning actual user needs and usage patterns.

NOTES

[1] Robert S. Taylor, *The Making of a Library: The Academic Library in Transition* (New York: Hayes and Becker, 1972), p. 83.

[2] James Thompson, *An Introduction to University Library Administration*, 2nd ed. (Hamden, CT: Linnet, 1974), p. 11.

[3] Taylor, *Making of a Library*, p. 83.

[4] Robert S. Taylor, "Patterns Toward a User-Centered Academic Library," in *New Dimensions for Academic Library Service*, ed. E. J. Josey (Metuchen, NJ: Scarecrow, 1975), p. 299.

[5] Taylor, *Making of a Library*, pp. 37-38.

[6] Rutherford D. Rogers and David C. Weber, *University Library Administration* (New York: H. W. Wilson, 1971), p. 113.

[7] Charles D. Churchwell, "The Library in Academia: An Associate Provost's View," in *New Dimensions in Academic Library Service*, p. 21.

[8] R. Dean Galloway and Zoia Horn, "Alternative Ways to Meet User Needs," in *New Dimensions in Academic Library Service*, pp. 121-22.

[9] Mary Carter, et al., *Building Library Collections*, 4th ed. (Metuchen, NJ: Scarecrow, 1974), p. 141.

[10] Connie R. Dunlap, "Organizational Patterns in Academic Libraries, 1876-1976," *College and Research Libraries* 37 (Summer 1976): 395-407.

[11] Ibid., pp. 397-98.

[12] Kevin Guinagh, "The Professor's Reliance on the Library," in *The Academic Library: Essays in Honor of Guy R. Lyle*, ed. Evan Farber and Ruth Walling (Metuchen, NJ: Scarecrow, 1974), p. 137.

[13] "Reference Standards," *RQ* 1 (June 1961): 1-2.

[14] William Katz, *Introduction to Reference Works* (New York: McGraw-Hill, 1969), 2:75.

[15] "Reference Standards," p. 1.

[16] J. McRee Elrod, "Is the Card Catalogue's Unquestioned Sway in North America Ending?" *Journal of Academic Librarianship* 2 (March 1976): 4.

[17] Ibid., p. 5.

[18] Charles R. McClure, "Subject and Added Entries as Access in Information," *Journal of Academic Librarianship* 2 (March 1976): 13-14.

[19] Joan K. Marshall, "A New Look at Organizing Materials in Academic Libraries," in *New Dimensions in Academic Library Service*, p. 132.

[20] Rogers and Weber, *University Library Administration*, p. 199.

[21] Joe Boisse, "An Opinion" in "Library Instruction: A Column of Opinion," ed. Carolyn Kirkendall, *Journal of Academic Librarianship* 2 (Sept. 1976): 188.

[22] See bibliography in Betty Young's work, which follows, pp. 124-25.

[23] Betty Young, "Circulation Services—Is It Meeting the User's Needs?" *Journal of Academic Librarianship* 2 (July 1976): 122.

[24] Ibid.

[25] Allan J. Dyson, "Organizing Undergraduate Library Instruction: The English and American Experience," *Journal of Academic Librarianship* 1 (March 1975): 12-13.

[26] Howard W. Dillon, "Organizing the Academic Library for Instruction," *Journal of Academic Librarianship* 1 (Sept. 1975): 6-7.

[27] Ibid., p. 4.

[28] Evan I. Farber, "College Librarians and the University Library Syndrome," in *The Academic Library*, p. 14.

[29] Ibid., pp. 16-17.

[30] Nancy Hammond, "Teaching Library Use," in *Libraries in Higher Education: The User Approach to Service*, ed. John Cowley (Handen, CT: Linnet, 1975), pp. 83-101.

[31] E. W. Erickson, "Government, Organization, and Administration," in *Reader in the Academic Library*, ed. Michael M. Reynolds (Washington: NCR Microcard Editions, 1970), p. 97.

[32] Dunlap, "Organizational Patterns in Academic Libraries," p. 399.

[33] Ibid., pp. 399-400.

[34] Taylor, *Making of a Library*, p. 131.

[35] Ibid.

[36] Daniel Gore, "Zero-Growth: When Is NOT-Enough Enough? A Symposium," *Journal of Academic Librarianship* 1 (Nov. 1975): 4-5.

[37] Taylor, *Making of a Library*, p. 131.

[38] Harold Opgrand, "An Evaluation of the Closed Reserve at St. Cloud State College" (Starred paper, University of Minnesota, 1961); Anthony C. Schulzetenberg, "An Evaluation of the Closed Reserve at St. Cloud State College: A Follow-Up Study" (Starred paper, University of Minnesota, 1968); Ford Jensen, "A Cost Analysis and Usage Study of the Reserved Materials Collection at the University of Arizona Main Library" (Starred paper, University of Arizona, 1971) [ERIC Nos. ED 060889, 060888, and 054822, respectively].

[39] R. Dean Galloway and Zoia Horn, "Alternative Ways to Meet User Needs," in *New Dimensions in Academic Library Service*, pp. 126-27.

[40] Guy R. Lyle, *The Administration of the College Library*, 4th ed. (New York: H. W. Wilson, 1974), p. 137; Rogers and Weber, *University Library Administration*, pp. 30-34.

[41] Paul Wasserman, *The New Librarianship: A Challenge for Change* (New York: Bowker, 1972), pp. 38-39.

[42] G. Edward Evans, *Management Techniques for Librarians* (New York: Academic Press, 1976), p. 190.

[43] Rogers and Weber, *University Library Administration*, p. 356.

[44] The Committee for New College, "Student Reactions to Study Facilities," in *Reader in the Academic Library*, pp. 299-316.

5

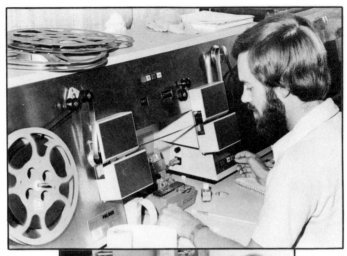

INSTRUCTIONAL TECHNOLOGY SERVICES

The scope and function of instructional technology services (ITS) as a unit varies greatly among academic institutions. Consequently, the services and division suggested here are made on the basis of a literature survey, personal experience, and a rather extensive overview of patterns observable throughout the United States. Prior to actual definition and discussion of the various areas encompassed by ITS, a graphic gestalt of ITS's implied structure through an organizational diagram may be helpful to consult (Figure 11).

Figure 11

Theoretical ITS Organizational Structure

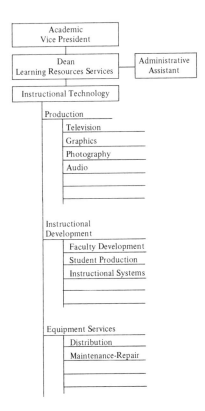

Although this suggested organizational structure is hypothetical, it is recommended by the authors. Certainly, other organizational structures may be used or the model may be adapted for local use. Paramount, however, in any ITS organization is that services be directed toward both instructional development and the production of materials. These services complement each other and rarely work well in isolation.

Experienced librarians and media specialists have for some time realized that needed curriculum materials are often not available on a commercial basis. When an unfulfilled request or a request satisfied by "the best we can find" occurs, frustrated media professionals realize how vulnerable they are when meeting the needs of the user. Attempts by early audiovisualists and librarians to cope with this frustration resulted in the creation of a production support services unit often found in academic libraries, media centers, learning resource centers, and audiovisual centers throughout the nation. The common term presently used to describe the systematic production of unique teaching-learning materials not available commercially is ITS.

It seems appropriate to define instructional technology both historically, as it has developed in many institutions today, and ideally, as the authors view it for the future. Although a plethora of definitions exists for instructional technology, the authors have chosen the two set forth by the *1970 Commission on Instructional Technology*:

> In its more familiar sense, it means the media born of the communications revolution which can be used for instructional purposes alongside the teacher, textbook, and blackboard. In general, the Commission's report follows this usage. In order to reflect present-day reality, the Commission has had to look at the pieces that make up instructional technology: television, films, overhead projectors, computers, and the other items of "hardware" and "software" (to use the convenient jargon that distinguishes machines from programs). In nearly every case, these media have entered education independently, and still operate more in isolation than in combination.
>
> The second and less familiar definition of instructional technology goes beyond any particular medium or device. In this sense, instructional technology is more than the sum of its parts. It is a systematic way of designing, carrying out, and evaluating the total process of learning and teaching in terms of specific objectives, based on research in human learning and communication, and employing a combination of human and nonhuman resources to bring about more effective instruction.[1]

The Commission found some similarities in each definition that should have meaning for the readers of a work such as this. They explained the breadth and depth of instructional technology as follows:

> Instructional technology, by either definition, includes a wide array of instruments, devices, and techniques, each with its particular problems, potential, and advocates. Note, however, that neither definition equates technology with "machines"—an easy mistake to make. To put prime emphasis on equipment—e.g., films, coaxial cable,

teaching machines—can lead up a blind alley. Many observers believe, for instance, that fascination with the gadgetry of instructional television to the exclusion of the idea behind it has often led to stereotyped and impoverished uses of that media.[2]

The authors view ITS within learning resources now much as the Commission saw instructional technology in 1970, in that two definitions and dimensions also exist today. Any attempt to bring higher education closer in line with the second definition lies within the realm of the learning resources concept. Within the framework of both definitions, then, this chapter is presented; however, it is within the spirit of the second definition that the authors find a working hypothesis for the development of this service within learning resources.

HISTORY

A cursory glance at the history of instructional technology reveals that there were two early tracks of development. The earliest track, known as the physical science concept (early 1900s), was largely confined to equipment distribution and aids to instruction; and it was referred to by numerous names and terms. Paul Saettler, in his book *A History of Instructional Technology*, mentioned a few of the various historical synonyms used to describe present ITS: "visual aids, teaching aids, audiovisual aids, visual instruction, audiovisual instruction, audiovisual materials, audiovisual communication, audiovisual technology."[3] The physical science concept was largely based on Comenian-Pestalozzian-Herbartian concepts, and is defined thus: "the application of physical science and engineering technology, such as motion picture projectors, tape recorders, television, teaching machines, for group presentation of instructional materials."[4]

The second track of development for instructional technology, called the behavioral science concept, found its initial roots in the latter half of the nineteenth century in the persons of E. B. Tylor, J. G. Frazer, Wilhelm Max Wundt, Alfred Binet, and B. Stanley Hall; but it received the impetus to develop into its present form at the beginning of World War I. Subsequent development of instructional technology occured between the two world wars as the need to examine psychology for the massive war effort became apparent. During the 1950s, through efforts of the Ford Foundation and the National Science Foundation, the behavioral science concept of instructional technology began a slow but steady movement toward maturity.[5] One of the best definitions of the behavioral science concept continues to be Saettler's:

Thus the basic view of the behavioral science concept of instructional technology is that educational practice should be more dependent on the methods of science as developed by behavioral scientists in the broad areas of psychology, anthropology, sociology, and in the more specialized areas of learning, group processes, language and linguistics, communications, administration, cybernetics, perception, and psychometrics.[6]

ATTITUDE

It is within the previously mentioned historical context, combining the theoretical and practical aspects of both definitions, that the authors recommend the organizational structure, services, and combination of functional areas outlined in this chapter. However, merely to develop an organizational structure for ITS within learning resources does not in and of itself provide a pattern for success. It is imperative for the director of a learning resource program to examine carefully two related factors, either of which may dictate success or failure of ITS as a unit thereof. Both deal with the development of attitude—one internal, one external; but without a clearly charted course, these two factors can develop attitudes unfavorable enough to seriously limit the performance of ITS as a unit. One is a commitment to an equality of format; the other involves the manner in which services are extended to the users of ITS. Consequently, consideration of these factors is crucial, and fuller exposition of each will preface this chapter's section on instructional development.

In-depth discussion of the individual services within ITS would be incomplete without some mention of attitude toward these services when contrasted with traditional print services. Although the entire range of attitudes toward all formats is discussed both implicitly and explicitly in other parts of the book, the authors feel compelled to mention again the necessity for equality of treatment of all formats at this departure. Mere acceptance or tolerance of formats other than print is simply not enough when subscribing to the learning resources concept. The formats and services organized with ITS are as essential to a twentieth century institution and faculty as are those other materials traditionally associated with the library.

An attitude toward photographic services such as that expressed by Thompson (although presumably not intending to be patronizing) is *not* conducive to either a healthy development of services or an attitude of equality for all formats. He stated:

> Such a service makes all slides and prints from books and manuscripts; it also photographs paintings and museum objects; and it does "location work"—that is, the photographers go out and photograph buildings, for example. In general, it provides the visual aids required by the university for teaching and research. There is no essential reason why such a service should be part of the library. There are indeed certain advantages: the library is itself a central service, usually in a central location, and this makes for convenience; and it is a safer situation where library materials do not have to leave the library premises to be photographed. But if, for example, a university sets up a central printing service, it would make much more sense if the university's photographic service was integrated with it, rather than left under the library's care.[7]

Another perception of the uses of various formats is one expressed by Robert Heinich:

Historically, audiovisual materials were designed to be used as a part of instruction, assuming a direct relationship to the teaching process, and planned for prior to instruction, whereas library services generally are called upon as a result of instruction by a classroom teacher. Even where book reference lists are drawn up in advance, the intent is use after instruction. Teachers use media; students use the library resources.[8]

Heinich makes here sharp distinctions concerning formats and utilization. Furthermore, such a distinction affects both conscious and unconscious attitudes toward differing treatment of a variety of materials.

The overriding thesis within ITS is one that does not presume *a* way to learn or *a* way to teach. ITS offers alternatives to the purely verbal strategy in the teaching-learning process. ITS theory presumes no hierarchy in teaching methodology or media format; rather it presumes individuality of learning and teaching styles. Therefore, a variety of media formats is essential.

Any further substantive discussion of ITS requires exploration of those financial policies and procedures governing the development, design, and production of instructional materials. Budgets at all levels are strained and stretched beyond their present capabilities now; therefore, learning resources staff will undoubtedly be searching for creative plans for financing all future services, including ITS. Any such plan should involve a critical look at cost accounting.

COST ACCOUNTING

There are several models for internal cost accounting, or internal chargeback, for materials and services offered from ITS to the university at large. Certainly, every college or university is faced with the problems that result from the distribution and disbursement of funds that have been allocated or must be collected or transferred. The operational definition of internal chargeback utilized in this work is:

Internal Chargeback—that aspect of cost accounting that allows an area, center, or service organization to collect internally or have transferred from other university departments or areas the funds for services.

There are probably as many methods and levels of internal chargeback as there are colleges and universities. Some institutions are budgeted in such a manner that their ITS area is allocated enough funding to pay for all materials and services rendered to faculty, students, and administrative staff; consequently, this requires little, if any, financial support from the requesting department or area. Other institutions charge the requesting department or area for all materials and services whether the amount used is large or small.

The intent of this section is to compare and contrast the two major approaches to internal cost accounting. The first method requires that all materials and services be charged back to the requesting department or area, regardless of amount. The second provides each person requesting services an established maximum dollar amount for those materials and services not charged back to the department. When the individual faculty member reaches this maximum amount, the department is consulted concerning the project and is requested to fund the amount in excess of the established maximum. This second system requires that the institution allocate sufficient monies to ITS when the initial institutional budget is established.

As with other issues where there are convincing data for several approaches, the authors have chosen to present arguments supporting major approaches, while recognizing that individual institutions will seek their own solutions based on existing circumstances. These considerations include personnel, the traditional political arena, budget constraints, and faculty usage.

Whether an institution uses an internal chargeback system in a very rigid manner or in some modified way, a thorough analysis of the advantages and disadvantages of each ought to be made. It is quite possible that the administrative convenience found in a rigid approach to an internal chargeback system may be offset by the fact that faculty well may be intimidated by budget constraints and pressure, and therefore fail to develop needed instructional materials. Likewise, the internal chargeback system chosen can promote or discourage departmental accountability. Establishing priorities for instructional or informational projects by department is a possible solution to the dilemma of choosing a system that provides accountability yet fosters creativity for development. There can be little doubt that the most rigid approach to internal chargeback is the easiest to manage and defend from a straight cost accounting point of view. It is not without disadvantage, however. Faculty members, with busy schedules, traditional approaches, and concern over budget restrictions, may lose interest in the development of materials or find the path to materials development replete with obstacles. Also, given the nature of college faculty and the academic propensity for the lecture method, setting project priorities can lead to extended time limits on development and production, or even elimination of innovative projects altogether.

Walk-in business is encouraged through the more flexible, maximum dollar approach to an internal chargeback system, even though it sometimes may be indicative of too little pre-planning. This inherent weakness is sometimes aggravated by a lack of financial accountability. Interestingly, when the hassles of bookkeeping, cost accounting, and computer printouts are reduced, a reluctance to request service is decreased. Moreover, walk-in business can frequently be directed toward better and more complex future projects and materials development.

The flexibility of the maximum dollar internal chargeback system may create an attitude on the part of faculty of experimentation with new and innovative techniques and materials, since every attempt at innovation is not charged back to an already extended budget. Likewise, other department members, chairpersons, or deans will be less likely to restrict faculty production of innovative materials through intimidation or discouragement. This is especially true of new faculty as well as those who are fledgling users. However, without some budget restrictions, depletion of departmental allocations by one faculty member is possible, thereby handicapping the respective department as well as the entire ITS area.

This problem can be kept to a minimum with sound policies and insightful management. Some approaches for dealing with overly enthusiastic faculty members, although involving perhaps nothing more than good common sense, are worth mentioning. Arbitrary financial limits (e.g., percentages based on total budget divided by total number of faculty) on materials and services for faculty members and departments have some merit. Faculty members who show interest and offer sound instructional ideas that might exceed the established maximum amount should be encouraged to meet with their departmental head and the director of ITS. These meetings should encourage the faculty members to explain fully the scope, sequence, goals, and objectives of their projects. Shared cost schemes between departments and ITS are an accountable and workable arrangement for cases of this sort. Similar policies can create rather than discourage further development. Likewise, departmental members, should they deem the projects worthwhile, have a greater commitment once involved.

The authors have proposed, in the previous discussion, some alleged advantages and disadvantages of a chargeback system from a library perspective. This has been done realizing that few institutions see this issue as binary; rather, they see it as a continuum, choosing to locate themselves somewhere between the extremes.

While the previous exposition of attitudes and finances is no recipe for success, attention given by the director to the development of both should reap dividends for the ITS and consequently for learning resources. An ITS organizational structure can then be developed that assures both internal and external support. Within that structure, and developed on the basis of instructional needs, an entire range of services can be provided. These services will be examined in some depth. The reader should note, however, before reading the discussion of ITS that follows, that in no case has an attempt been made to discuss instructional and production techniques. This omission was by design, since the major goals and subsequent objectives of this book are to address the integration, organization, and administration of materials and possible services, and not specific techniques. Underlying any good ITS program is an instructional development unit. Primary attention will next be directed toward an analysis of the scope and functions of a typical instructional development subdivision.

INSTRUCTIONAL DEVELOPMENT

Definitions of instructional development abound, especially in the educational periodical literature of the early 1970s. The authors, after several years of actual experience in the *process* of instructional development, have chosen two definitions that are somewhat dated but valid and wide enough in combined scope to relate the intended meaning. The first definition is:

... a systematic process of defining and using relevant instructional goals to create effective learning activities.[9]

Instructional development is essentially pragmatic, eclectic and behavioristic. It is pragmatic in that it focuses on what works whether or not an adequate explanation exists. It is eclectic drawing from a number of disciplines including, but not limited to, psychology, social psychology, sociology, management, anthropology and communications. ID is in the enviable position of not being a classical discipline which must defend its boundaries. Rather it is free to draw from whatever sources are useful. It is behavioristic in that it focuses on students learning and the observation of student behavior. It is not grounded in any specific learning theory, but draws from a variety of behavioristic learning theories. The criterion is, "Is it useful?"[10]

Whatever the source, the authors are convinced that any viable definition of instructional development must recognize instructional development as a *process*. Any definition should include these essential elements: 1) improvement of instruction, 2) systematic approach, 3) cognizance of all resources, 4) goal orientation, and 5) instructional materials orientation (all formats).

Both the concept and the process of instructional development will be covered in chapter six; however, the authors have chosen to discuss it within the ITS chapter as well, recognizing that these services are frequently found in this area. Such services are often offered from ITS whether that division is located within learning resources or included in another organizational area.

Instructional development services should include, but not be limited to, services ranging from simple assistance with the use of single items of one format to complex help with several items in many formats. The service should range from assistance with daily walk-in business to comprehensive unit, course, and program development and redevelopment.

As is true in many cases, the placement of instructional development services varies within administrative patterns and configurations from one college to another. Although the authors find instructional development most compatible within the learning resources model, further development of various organizational and administrative arrangements are recognized as being potentially interesting, academically sound, and organizationally effective. Since ITS serves the entire campus with necessary production services, it also seems both instructionally sound and cost-effective to include either a section of instructional development within ITS or to make the entire instructional development arm as part and parcel of the area. Various sections of ITS (e.g., graphics, photography, audio, motion picture, television, etc.) are all essential in the production of materials, most of which are instructional in nature. It is quite sound as well to have these materials reviewed, discussed, designed, developed, and possibly referred to a professional developer during the various stages of their production.

Instructional development—not unlike religion, politics, and war—has nearly as many definitions and derivatives as it has proponents and opponents. Minimal services offered from an ITS area could incorporate the principles of good instructional design into locally produced instructional materials. Beyond this, the application of principles of systematic programming to transparencies, slides, slide/tapes, talking books, and still photography presentations would seem invaluable, if not a necessity. Production of materials is nearly impossible without some attention to instructional development and design, so it is organizationally feasible to establish production service units within ITS.

Services of instructional unit development, course development, and program development are desirable at the onset of establishing learning resource services; they are essential after two years of operation. Instructional design services as applied to single- and multiple-media items and formats are essential at the initial organization of learning resource services and ITS.

Instructional Graphics

Instructional graphics is more than art work and illustration for slides, transparencies, posters, etc. Instructional graphics is in essence the front line of the entire production effort in ITS. The result of that effort is what you see; it represents an attempt to visualize concepts, people, feelings, ideas, moods, and products. Graphics is commercial art in every sense of the word and being so, it reflects the visual culture of the times. The lasting power and significance of commercial art (and, in the authors' opinion, its stepchild, instructional graphics) was attested to by Lou Dorfsman in his introduction to *Graphis Annual 73/74*:

> The ideas and the transcendent issues of an era have always been powerfully reflected by its art. And, according to the critic Ruskin, truthfully reflected: "Great nations write their autobiographies in three manuscripts—the book of their deeds, the book of their words and the book of their art. Not one of these books can be understood unless we read the two others, but of the three the only trustworthy one is the last."
>
> And in my view it is no stretch or distortion of meaning to include commercial art as a category under Art-with-a-capital-A.
>
> Is commercial art created to order and based on subjects dictated by an outside source? So was much of the work of the Renaissance. It is occupied with industrial processes and social comment. Painters have been painting iron foundries since as far back as Hieronymus Bosch, who of course came from one of the first parts of Europe to become industrialized. No less a poet than Wordsworth saw a poem in the arrival of a night shift at a factory. And need I mention Dickens' "Nicholas Nickleby" and "Hard Times"?[11]

Graphics, our visual language, constantly change, and a functional instructional graphics laboratory should be in tune with trends, fads, and visual symbolism, both national and international, in order to create the kinds of images, moods, and ideas needed for the rest of the visual services of ITS. The necessity for change in the graphic arts in order to remain fresh and responsive to national and international languages within graphics was commented on by Jerome Snyder in introducing *Graphis Annual 74/75*:

> Visual language, more so than other languages, is in a constant state of flux. While a formal or written tongue is confined largely to its national enclave and customs, graphic and visual concepts are exported and imported with little or no hindrance from national barriers or cultural tariffs. Trading of graphic styles, techniques, visual idioms, colloquialisms, is dependent primarily on the accessability and easy exchange of information. . . . If technology is reshaping life-styles throughout the world, it also has made differing societies more adaptable to new modes of graphic expression. To be sure, the graphic stream does not flow evenly, untrammelled, or at the same speed in all parts of the world. Necessity does not quite exercise the same motherhood in all

places at all times. Graphic invention and ingenuity are not spawned equally or universally. But the printed page, the poster, the film, television, wherever the artist/designer lays a graphically ingenious hand, all are the bearers of crossbreeding ideas and styles.[12]

An efficient graphics lab needs creativity, organization, sensitive supervision, and adequate space. Although this chapter does not intend, other than implicity, to discuss personnel, the authors feel they would be remiss (since instructional graphics tends to bring together diverse creative people) not to mention the intangible of personnel supervision in instructional graphics.

Graphic services can range from complex animation cells to simple posters and preservation techniques. The essential ingredients are simple to describe, yet often difficult to locate and combine in a formula that will afford success. Graphics labs in colleges offer to the entire academic community their services of illustration, preservation, reproduction, and transparency production, etc.

Photography

The photography section of ITS may offer services from sophisticated cinematography and color processing to accepting simple photographic orders that will be processed by a local photo retailer. The degree of local sophistication and comprehensiveness depends on both time available and item totals within the sub-sections of photography. The break-even point between in-house services and commerical services will vary with local competition, the population of the surrounding area, the college's or state's bidding procedures, and the availability of technical expertise (student help and professional staff). If the college or university offers emphasis in photojournalism, photo technology, or cinematography, shared professional and technical staff may be a possibility. This availability may influence greatly the types and comprehensiveness of services offered. Programs of this type will also dictate to a large degree the competencies available with the student body, which may be a very important variable in the decision to offer selected services that rely on student help.

At the very minimum, learning resource services, through ITS, should offer faculty an area to which black and white film, color slides, and motion picture film can be brought for processing. Processing may be handled in a variety of ways. Photographic copy work, as well as some on-site photographic services, should also be minimum services offered even in a new organization.

Slide duplication, black and white and color processing, and product photography, if not required within still photography services, are at least expected by most faculty and administration. Slide duplication, black and white processing, and product photography can not usually be done cost effectively on a commercial basis outside of the institution. Therefore, these services should also be considered essential.

Most ITS areas offer some type of motion picture service. If the minimum services of receiving orders for processing, advising faculty on the advisability of cinema, and film splicing are offered, then variables of cost, turn around time, and quality control in the processing lab should be carefully analyzed. Quality and services offered by commercial processors of both still and motion film vary greatly and require competitive shopping.

Filmmaking as a service requires a commitment that many colleges have not been willing to make in the past. Largely, this hesitancy is due to the cost of personnel, space, and equipment. While quality motion picture service requires a solid institutional commitment, many colleges have made modest moves in the direction of motion picture production. Moreover, a number of these colleges have chosen to invest in super 8 equipment. This may largely be due to technological breakthroughs and advances in super 8 technology, since a large percentage of super 8 equipment presently available is comparable to that of its predecessors, 35mm and 16mm. This suggests that motion picture services may no longer be outside the financial reach of most institutions.

Any college or university considering motion picture production should ensure institutional commitment in terms of finances and goals; then, having a defined commitment, size of format becomes a critical consideration. If motion picture production is prohibitive for a college, the plans for alternatives must be well conceived.

Audio

Audio services can be divided functionally into two subdivisions—reproduction and production. Reproduction of existing materials and production of newly created or designed materials each require some unique facilities and equipment; however, they also contain many common elements. In learning resources, the similarities exceed the differences by a large enough margin to justify integration of both in terms of physical location and supervision.

Reproduction facilities should be capable of offering to students and faculty the services of either duplicating materials in the same format (e.g., cassette to cassette) or converting materials from one to another (e.g., phono disc to cassette). The services listed below are those that could be expected from most audio service areas:

1. phono disc or record to reel or cassette
2. cassette to reel and vice-versa
3. multiple copies from any of the above conversions
4. high speed duplication of both reel and cassette

Audio production units often consist of very complex and sophisticated facilities and equipment that may be at the level of studio broadcast or near broadcast quality. If the studio production area supports, or is part of, the college radio station, its equipment and services might be quite different from those found in an ITS area serving campus instructional program needs. (The authors are assuming the college radio station to be located under other administrative jurisdiction within the college when describing services and facilities.)

The following capabilities should be expected in audio production:

1. *Space*—audio production studio, or separate physical area for sound recording. Preferably this area should be soundproofed and acoustically treated to reduce extraneous noise and allow the producer to obtain maximum fidelity. Hardware should be physically separated from the recording booth.

2. *Editing*—capability should be sophisticated enough to allow for the addition to, or removal of, sentences, words, or syllables within locally or commercially produced tapes.

3. *Mixing*—capacity for mixing more than one audio signal from several like or different sources should be available in order to create high quality, professional sound productions.

The degree to which the institution's long range goals are met through music and foreign language programs may dictate the quality of audio production and reproduction in which the ITS area chooses to become involved. Good quality audio productions and reproductions are not only desirable but required for effectively listening to comprehensive and complex instructional material. Therefore, high quality audio equipment and facilities are essential in serving students and faculty requesting audio services from learning resources.

Equipment Services

Distribution of educational hardware or equipment for both permanent and temporary loans has long been a campus service in institutions of higher education. This service has been and continues to be offered from numerous areas within the university. Among the areas where equipment and educational hardware have been offered for use are audiovisual services, audiovisual centers, film libraries, student centers or unions, and libraries. Although various locations for equipment services have existed and will continue to exist, their overall objective and development have followed similar trends regardless of physical location.

The stereotyped "library complex" of collect, centralize, and check out has been one definite, identifiable trend within equipment services regardless of location. This pattern has been followed under some assumptions that were not altogether without merit, as follows:

1. Centralized purchasing affords more competitive prices.

2. Centralized equipment pools provide ease for both preventive and major maintenance.

3. Centralized equipment collections allow for standardization of brand names and models.

4. Good relationships between media specialists assigned to equipment services and faculty borrowing equipment from a centralized pool can result in increased use and often provides for instructional development "in-roads."

5.   Centralization curbs the possessiveness that some departments have
a tendency to develop toward equipment checked out to them on
long-term loan.

During the years 1965-1975, electronic equipment of all types became part
of the overall trappings of youth throughout the United States, which had a
tendency to modify, if not completely change, the attitudes of professional media
personnel toward centralization. As equipment losses and breakdowns increased
during the late 1960s and early 1970s, media personnel were forced to take another
look at the centralization concept. True, equipment losses and vandalism have been
coped with in a variety of ways. However, the re-thinking of centralization and how
this re-thinking has manifested itself is of major importance here. Many colleges
have chosen to maintain centralized purchasing and a small accompanying centralized equipment collection, which usually assures centralized maintenance and
repair.

As an alternative to large equipment pools within learning resources, many
colleges have placed rather complete equipment inventories within each school
and/or department. The departmental inventory of equipment is generally placed
in a secure location, but one accessible to the respective faculty. These satellite collections may have an informal checkout procedure, or in small departments, policies
of "first come, first served" may prevail. This approach usually requires the dean
and/or department chairperson, and subsequently the faculty, to assume an active
responsibility for their equipment inventory. The rather obvious advantage to this
method lies in its simple but effective method of accountability. Faculty suddenly
have to answer to the dean and department chairpersons for lost or stolen equipment that they might have recently used. They also have to live with the conse-
quences of decreases in other budget areas if they choose to replace lost equipment.
Another not so attractive alternative for the faculty member after departmental
equipment is lost is the option of checking out equipment from a reduced but
centralized collection within learning resource services. This presents more of a problem to the faculty member since less equipment is available; and it requires the
effort of picking up and returning equipment. This approach to portable equipment,
although not without some disadvantages, shows considerable promise for the future.

Television

Portable TV equipment should be handled in equipment services, where
equipment such as cameras, videotape recorders (VTRs), tripods, monitors, port-
a-pack units, and the various accompanying patch cords should be available for
checkout on both a short- and long-term basis. This portable equipment need have
little direct connection with television services as an area within ITS. Consequently,
this dimension will not be taken up here other than to say that it should be handled
like all other portable equipment.

Television, more than any other service of learning resources, requires both a
solid, sound institutional commitment, and it must have a positive correlation with
the institution's long range goals and objectives. Television is expensive! It is expensive in every possible phase, from equipment to personnel. However, television is
necessary for quality higher education, and it is financially feasible for every

institution if carefully planned for and utilized for its unique format characteristics. This is to say that television can be invaluable as a unique addition to the record of knowledge.

Numerous television installations indicate that creative and effective uses of the medium can be made where both modest and extravagant capital outlay are involved. This does not lead to any hard conclusions on television investment versus quality production; but it does appear, after a not so cursory glance, that quality television production output is not completely a function of financial investment.

Television services vary according to each institution's needs, commitment and goals, history, and leadership. Those television services found in higher education today may range from simple remodeled classrooms equipped with cameras, VTRs, lights, etc., to broadcast-quality studio facilities (such as Newhouse II, the new Television Radio Center at Syracuse University where 8,000 square feet of floor space is devoted to television studio space alone).[13]

As is the case with many services offered in learning resources, the authors recommend a middle-of-the-road commitment to television, unless there is substantial evidence that a greater or lesser investment is clearly indicated. "Middle-of-the-road" here reflects the following services and space:

A. Services

1. Off-air recording capability.

2. Video tape reproduction capability.

3. Program production capability of:
    a. observation of tapes from various sources (e.g., guest lectures, student teachers, student performances in speech, music, drama, etc.)

    b. production of programming that assists in college courses and in some cases provides the major portion of instruction in those courses.

B. Space

1. Color studio production space with soundproofing, and adequate ceiling height for lighting grids.

2. Separate control rooms.

3. Storage for extra equipment and a minimum number of sets and extra furniture.

A discussion of television would be incomplete without a final note mentioning the place of instructional development in television production. Television programming for instructional use lacks a pivotal dimension without a pre-designed instructional development effort. The programming should be systematically planned and developed, with the package aimed at meeting carefully identified instructional objectives. Such programming should be pretested on the intended audience, revised where necessary, and then re-evaluated after moving out of the prototype stage. Careful collection of data should be done to measure student success and attitudes toward television programming, and this can be used for program revision where necessary. Finally, every effort should be made so that there is some assurance that television is indeed the appropriate format for attacking the instructional problem and meeting the instructional objectives.

ITS for Students

The concept of providing ITS for students is congruous with the learning resources concept in every sense of the word. Students and faculty alike use services of reference, periodicals, and circulation; therefore, to expect different treatment in services of audio, photography, and graphics would be inconsistent. The question is not whether services should be available, but rather at what level and with what financial base.

The authors' position is that ITS for students should be a modest replica of those services offered to the rest of the college. Translated into specifics, this requires that space, equipment, and assistance be available to students in the following areas:

A. Photography
    1. copystands
    2. cameras (35mm with appropriate lenses and filters)

B. Preservation
    1. drymounting
    2. laminating
    3. ventilated area
        a. adhesives
        b. brush-on materials
        c. protective coatings

C. Audio
    1. conversion of format
    2. production
    3. reproduction
        a. record to tape
        b. reel to cassette and vice-versa

D. Preview samples of material in all available formats

E. Graphics
    1. transparency production
    2. signs and posters
    3. simple lettering techniques

F. Multiple-format production (e.g., slide-tape)

The long-range rationale, goals, and benefits of ITS for students come largely from the society changing as a result of technology. Students arrive at colleges today with experiences, competencies, and expectations that are quite different from their counterparts of previous decades. Students in both elementary and secondary schools have not only experienced using materials in a variety of formats but also have been expected to produce them for presentations in their classes. They have seen a variety of instructional materials used to communicate, and many of them have already had photography courses. Furthermore, colleges today are squarely amidst the television generation, and students are much more visually oriented than students of the 1950s and 1960s. Still another factor is the revolution that many public libraries have experienced with regard to media formats other than print. In short, students are accustomed to a variety of services both as a convenience and as another means of communicating their ideas.

Financing materials used in production can be complex at best and difficult at worst. One option is for merchants and/or bookstores to stock and sell, in small quantities and at reasonable prices, the necessary stock for production. A second option is for the student area of ITS to sell raw stock directly to students for their production needs. This is only possible where there are no restraints placed on the LRC by the college administration, state purchasing agency, or college charter. Still another option, which is in reality an outgrowth of the second one mentioned, is the barter-card system. Using this system, students purchase a card for a given amount of money, and then through a punch system they "purchase" slide film, poster board, drymount tissue, transparency film, etc., with their card until the card has been rendered spent.

The last option offers some distinct advantages to students. These are realized largely through better prices, since the college can buy in volume and, hence, charge lower prices when retailing the materials. The second advantage is convenience, since students can complete their projects without leaving campus or for that matter, the center, should they be doing research there for a class or project. A third advantage lies in the development of a positive attitude toward the entire center and its services. Availability of the materials "in-house" gives students the feeling of complete service, which reduces hassles and improves overall attitudes toward the center and its services.

SUMMARY

This chapter offers a perspective on ITS that encompasses a wide variety of services. It incorporates those areas historically referred to as audiovisual services, in addition to the expanded aspect of developing and designing instruction and choosing the appropriate media format. The definitions referred to earlier in the Commission Report, accompanied by the behavioral science dimension of instructional technology referred to by Saettler, are essential to the direction of this chapter. When commenting on the potential place of instructional technology in learning, Sidney G. Tickton (in his book *To Improve Learning: An Evaluation of Instructional Technology*) quotes Alfred North Whitehead when expressing a view that this chapter and book support:

Instructional technology can help to bridge the gap between the world outside and the world inside the school. Television and xerography can bring immediacy to the learner. They can make possible a dynamic curriculum. If instructional technology is creatively applied, the student's route to knowledge and understanding can be more direct.

Knowledge and reality, filtered through the words of textbook and teacher, all too often reach the student as predigested conclusions, neatly packaged, and thoroughly divorced from what Alfred North Whitehead called the "radically untidy, ill-adjusted character" of reality.

"First-hand knowledge," Whitehead wrote, "is the ultimate basis of intellectual life. To a large extent book-learning conveys second-hand information, and as such can never rise to the importance of immediate practice. Our goal is to see the immediate events of our lives as instances of our general ideas."[14]

Tickton comments further on the limits of technology, saying:

Technology does not have to move people; it transmits the impact of people. The limits to improving instruction through technology are political, parochial, financial—they are not inherent in technology itself.[15]

Services of instructional development, graphics, photography, audio, television, equipment distribution, and student production services should be available to faculty, administrators and students. All should be included within the concept of the learning resources and should offer the user more than hardware and instructional materials. Moreover, they should include those added services that allow instructional technology to penetrate into both the learning process and instructional strategy. (Also, while this work does not specify particular space requirements for any area of ITS, the reader is referred to *Criteria for Planning the College and University Learning Resources Center.*[16])

The Carnegie Commission adapted criteria from the Commission on Instructional Technology (of the Research and Development Office of the National Association of Education Broadcasters) when identifying the role of instructional technology. They suggested that two discreet, concrete tests should be made for improving instruction and creating confidence in technology:

The teaching-learning task to be performed should be essential to the course of instruction to which it is applied.
The task to be performed could not be performed as well—if at all—for the students served without the technology contemplated.[17]

This chapter has been written in the spirit of these criteria.

NOTES

[1] Commission on Instructional Technology, *A Report to the President and the Congress of the United States* (Washington: Government Printing Office, 1970), p. 19.

[2] Ibid., p. 20.

[3] Paul Saettler, *A History of Instructional Technology* (New York: McGraw-Hill, 1968), p. 3.

[4] Ibid., p. 2.

[5] Ibid.

[6] Ibid., p. 5.

[7] James Thompson, *An Introduction to University Library Administration*, 2nd ed. (Hamden, CT: Linnet, 1970), p. 124.

[8] Robert Heinich, *Technology and the Management of Instruction* (Washington: Association for Educational Communications and Technology, 1970), pp. 163-64.

[9] Dale G. Hamreus, "Toward a Definition of Instructional Development," (Paper delivered at the 1971 Association for Educational Communications and Technology Convention, Philadelphia, PA, March 1971), p. 1.

[10] Kent L. Gustafson, "Toward a Definition of Instructional Development," (Paper, Michigan State University, n.d.), p. 1.

[11] Lou Dorfsman, "Introduction," *Graphis Annual 73/74*, ed. Walter Herdeg (New York: Hastings House, 1973), p. 7.

[12] Jerome Snyder, "Introduction," *Graphis Annual 74/75*, ed. Walter Herdeg (New York: Hastings House, 1974), p. 7.

[13] Carol Sanders, "For Teaching Broadcasters: A Superb Television Production Plant," *Broadcast Management Engineering* 11 (Nov. 1975): 30.

[14] Sidney G. Tickton, ed., *To Improve Learning: An Evaluation of Instructional Technology*, 2 vol. (New York: Bowker, 1970-1971), 1:34.

[15] Ibid., 1:35.

[16] Irving A. Merrill and Harold A. Drob, *Criteria for Planning the College and University Learning Resources Center* (Washington: Association for Educational Communications and Technology, 1977).

[17] The Carnegie Commission on Higher Education, *The Fourth Revolution: Instructional Technology in Higher Education* (New York: McGraw-Hill, 1972), p. 11.

6

INSTRUCTIONAL DEVELOPMENT AND FACULTY DEVELOPMENT

Perhaps the most penetrating question that must be addressed in this chapter is whether or not instructional development (ID) belongs in learning resources. The hypothesis is that not only does it belong, but that it is also by definition a natural function of the learning resources concept. When relating ID, and in some respects faculty development, to the earlier chapters of this book, it should be clear that the authors presuppose an integral relationship between the LRC and both the college's goals and objectives and its instructional program. The realization that ID and faculty development lie squarely within the LRC concept reveals some rather far-reaching, infrequently considered implications.

The instructional development section of chapter five examined the reasons for inclusion of ID within that division of learning resources and presented some possible definitions of it. This chapter will expand that discussion, offering more breadth and depth to the concept and process of ID and its relationship to faculty development.

INSTRUCTIONAL DEVELOPMENT

ID is an interdisciplinary, eclectic, continuous, and systematic process leading to the improvement of instruction and often to the individualization and self-pacing thereof. Although definitions of ID are many and varied, suffice it to say that the common threads of systematic development, process, instructional improvement, instructional materials, evaluation, and individualization will be found in most definitions. A useful definition is found in an instructional development booklet used at SUNY's Oswego College of Arts and Sciences:

> The Office of Learning Resources is charged with promoting the increased effectiveness and efficiency of teaching and learning. It is to provide a variety of options to support traditional classroom activities and to encourage the use of alternate learning modes that are most

appropriate to help accomplish the goals of all academic programs and other designated institutional obligations. This office also directs liaison activities between the faculty and the Learning Resources agencies and among agencies themselves.[1]

The discussion of ID in chapter five was primarily a thumbnail sketch of the parameters of instructional development and design from the perspective of materials production. That introduction focused on definitions of development and design insofar as ID is considered a logical arm of ITS. Also, the authors were careful to note that several models for instructional development exist, along with several organizational structures for its inclusion within the university structure.

The two most prominent ID models found in use and discussed in the literature today are the product development model and the organizational model. Both are used and useful, and depend largely on one's perspective when considering their respective contributions. The product development model offers the developer the most assistance since it addresses the instructional aspects of objectives, strategy, activities, evaluation, feedback, and instructional materials. It is also based on empirical data. The organizational model, on the other hand, is largely local in origin and pertains to line-and-staff relationships within the particular college or university. This is not to say that these models are not important, since they probably spell ultimate success to the faculty member and the program.

It is imperative to note one possible liability in locating the ID component of the college within the learning resources structure. This is the result of the seemingly inherent human characteristic of providing solutions to instructional problems based on existing and available *resources* rather than on actual *symptoms and needs*. If media solutions are the most accessible, and if the developer is most familiar with them, then the possibility of both excessive and inappropriate media solutions offered to instructional problems exists. This is not to say that preconceived media solutions to all instructional problems can't be avoided; rather, it is to say that if and when ID sections or centers are located in LRCs, careful attention must be given to ensure unbiased solutions to instructional problems. If the use of media in one or more formats is the logical and agreed-upon solution, it should be done; however, when alternative methodology or restructuring of course components are the best instructional solution, then these must be pointed out and pursued.

The authors are careful to point out this potential liability of offering ID services within the learning resources concept, primarily because most authorities in the area are in agreement that ID has its origins in the instructional technology field. A further step in this genealogy will reveal that the audiovisual field is only a generation removed from ID and, therefore, ID is often criticized by skeptics as just another attempt at good audiovisual utilization. This may well be a legitimate criticism, and in order to have an exemplary ID program, these possible shortcomings bear noting and careful scrutiny.

If the path to ID services is fraught with possible misunderstanding and potential problems, then a more critical analysis of ID seems to be in order. The ID function and its relationship to the learning resources concept needs reiteration in order to establish a comprehensive rationale for the concept's inclusion in learning resources. Instructional development, as mentioned earlier, has as its goal improvement of instruction and learning through systematic design. This systematic process often takes the form of materials selection in all formats, along with a variety of methods and fresh activities for use with these materials. The authors have repeatedly addressed the learning resources concept in the context of terms and phrases like learning, curriculum, instruction, service, and student learning. Oswego's statement of purpose for learning resources offered an excellent contribution highlighting the integration of learning resources with instructional development:

> Instructional development is a systematic, continuous process that will assist educators in developing the most effective and efficient learning experiences for students. During the process, the widest variety of teaching-learning options possible are identified, with selections made based upon the expected learning outcomes.[2]

Inclusion of ID services within the learning resources model is certainly not completely unique. Several colleges and universities have structured or founded them within existing learning resources services. Notable examples are Utah State University and St. Cloud State University, which moved in that direction as early as 1971. The correlation between the purpose of ID and the basic goals of the learning resources concept is more than noteworthy; it is to some degree intellectually profound.

Once the definition of ID has been established, the reader may well ask why ID is needed at all. The question goes well beyond any definition, at least in the historical and sociological senses. It is a question deeply rooted in higher education—in its history, its evaluation, and its training of professors (the authors consciously use here the term professors and not teachers).

The genealogy of colleges can be traced through several historical lineages. One can look to the Chinese and Confucius, the Brahmanic Colleges of India, or to their counterparts in the European Middle Ages when searching for the origins of present higher education. The purpose of this discussion, however, is simply to look to those early historical examples for clues that might illuminate the way for instructional development's becoming an integral part of the learning resources concept. Moreover, one of the original purposes, and to some degree the one remaining common purpose, among institutions of higher education bears examination. That purpose is the communication of knowledge and ideas. It hardly needs mentioning that the universities of the past, whether Medieval European or Chinese, were significantly different from the modern Western university, which still shares some common ground with its ancestors, although primarily in the sharing of ideas and materials and in passing on traditions and culture.

In the historical context of communicating and sharing ideas, the learning resources concept and the inclusion of ID within it have not only a place but also a clearly established position within higher education. Essentially, the authors believe that teaching has been and continues to be one of the priorities of higher education; and since ID is clearly an effort that aims at improving teaching and learning, then its place within the learning resources concept is well founded.

The preparation of college professors demands some attention in light of ID. Basically, colleges attempt to pass on to future generations the culture's tradition as well as basic skills, appreciation, and professional preparation. They do this with a cadre of professors who are often ill-prepared as teachers, if indeed they are prepared at all. Also worth mentioning at this point is the fact that large percentages of these professors have communicated information, ideas, skills, values, attitudes, and knowledge for all their lives via the lecture method.

When discussing college faculty and their realization of what the public wants from colleges and their teachers, C. Robert Pace offered Harry Truman's oft quoted "If you can't stand the heat get out of the kitchen." Pace further stated that college faculty not only rarely get in the kitchen, but also would rather spend their time in the living room or the library.[3] When commenting on university teaching, Norman K. Henderson lamented the experience, methods, and efficiency of teaching in higher education:

> In a period of rapid expansion the universities take in large numbers of new staff, often inexperienced in teaching and in need of training . . . little consideration has so far been given anywhere to a candidate's teaching ability, to his personal qualities and the suitability of his relationships with students.
>
> How efficient has university teaching been in the past under this system, for example in using lecturing as a means of instruction? Some estimates place this procedure very low in effectiveness if the purpose is to impart meaningful facts. It is a case of not only who will teach whom, but of who will first accept being taught how to teach.
>
> Some of the best teaching takes place in infant schools and kindergartens. But as we go up through the primary and secondary schools it seems to deteriorate; and when we come to the university it appears that it no longer matters at all! This is reflected in the long period of professional training required of infant and kindergarten teachers (usually 3 years), with less time for training primary teachers (generally 2 years), and one year of professional preparation required of secondary teachers, and none whatsoever for university lecturers![4]

Critics of both college teaching and the preparation of college teachers are in abundance, and a veritable smorgasbord of opinions will satisfy even the most subtle of appetites. One could start with William James's classic *Memories and Studies*, referring specifically to "The Ph.D. Octopus" section, and sample several works in the Jossey-Bass Series in Higher Education and arrive at a single conclusion: college teachers are given little career guidance when entering the profession and are given very little formal training in how to teach. Mainly, they teach as they were taught and are given little assistance either before or after becoming professors.

Most applicable to this work is a comment made by Mark Mancall (taken from the 1969 self-study, *The Study of Education at Stanford* and reported by Kenneth E. Eble in his book *Professors as Teachers*). Mancall stated that "What is most remarkable about the history of graduate education in the United States is that many of the same problems and issues have been raised decade after decade, with no real solution forthcoming."[5] This is a particularly cogent comment because it goes squarely to the heart of the argument for both instructional and faculty development in general and for their inclusion in learning resources. At the risk of sounding cynical, the authors have found little evidence that systematic or perceptive change has taken place in faculty preparation since Mancall made his statement in 1969.

Further documentation on the level and type of pedagogical preparation professors received in their pursuit of college teaching is available from many sources, and complete research in the area of college faculty preparation for teaching will not be attempted in this work. Rather, a representative sample of the literature will be examined to establish the case for lack of preparation in methodology, communication skill, and human relations skills for college faculty members.

When commenting on personal development of faculty members after they are hired, and the emphasis placed on that development in most colleges, Eble quoted a study by Miller and Wilson:

> We are left with a variety of practices of lesser significance: financial assistance for attendance at professional meetings, conferences, or workshops, or visiting lecturers, or consultants on teaching; load adjustments for research and writing; lighter loads for first-year faculty members, and particularly, at small colleges, financial assistance for further graduate work.[6]

In 1968, Milton and Shoben commented:

> College teaching is probably the only profession in the world for which no specific training is required. The profession of scholarship is rich in prerequisites for entry, but not that of instruction.[7]

Eble's findings of 1972 are paralleled by Miller and Wilson's earlier (1960) work and serve to further document the lack of systematic pedagogical training or retraining for professors. He stated:

> Except for favorable treatment shown to the first-year teacher, none of these practices directly affect teaching. Attendance at some professional meetings might well enhance teaching; attendance at others would contribute little. The standard way of getting travel money is to read a paper at a professional meeting, a practice useful enough to research but in some ways harmful to teaching. The presupposition in most of these practices is that development of greater command over a subject matter will contribute to the faculty member's general competence, of which teaching is one aspect. . . . Few schools pay any conscious attention to the ways in which faculty members develop, sustain their efforts, or decline.[8]

Jerry Gaff, commenting on college teaching in 1975, said:

> In their more candid moments, most faculty members readily confess that they learned to teach by being thrown into the classroom and either swimming or sinking; almost all will testify to doing considerable thrashing about before discovering how to swim. And even yet some go under. Given the new realities of higher education, this "do nothing" approach is not sufficient. Whatever its merits may have been, the call to hire good people and get out of their way becomes a hollow slogan when student enrollments dip, faculty positions are trimmed, and the very survival of some institutions is threatened.[9]

Suffice it to say that the necessity for instructional development is very evident, as illustrated in the previous statements and quotations. Beyond these comments, though, it should be understood that instructional development works not only toward teaching but also toward student learning; and where teaching and student learning are considered, methodology as well as faculty development must also be considered. Every institution must face the fact that they have on their faculties serious, dedicated professionals, many of whom *can* teach and most of whom *want* to teach, but many of whom lack the tools, the background, or the time to do adequate, much less excellent, jobs in teaching.

The reason for instructional development rests squarely on the premise that instruction needs improvement and that that improvement can be accomplished through the process of instructional development. Faculty members need exposure to instructional development as a process that addresses the teacher, the learning process, content, methods, and learning materials in all formats. Within this context, the authors find a rationale for including instructional development services within the learning resources concept. Learning resources in its specific and more general senses addresses the learning of both students and faculty through all available resources. Resources, as previously defined, are aimed at the improvement of instruction through instructional development and are considered within the confines of the learning resources concept.

FACULTY DEVELOPMENT

The most significant and obvious difference between faculty development (FD) and ID probably can be found within the realm of procedures and expectations. ID is systematic in its approach, with well defined goals and objectives. Many writers have insisted on emphasizing that ID is a goal-oriented *process* for the improvement of instruction. ID is usually a team effort with a well-defined audience. However, although faculty development may be systematic in the broadest sense, its goals and objectives are not always as well defined and may be more institutional than specifically audience-related. Leadership for FD is often the responsibility of one or more designated people who arrange for a variety of experiences and activities for interested faculty members. The goals of many FD programs as a matter of fact are explicitly faculty oriented and implicitly student oriented.

When contrasted with ID, FD takes on a more personal characteristic, in that it emphasizes personal renewal, updating of subject matter, and most especially, personal growth and development. FD should be designed to encourage faculty to a gradual but eventually dramatic metamorphasis in personal methodology, subject matter competence, and individual understanding of themselves, their students, the student-faculty relationship, and the interface between subject matter and people.

FD is by no means a new concept; however, it has taken on a new dimension since 1970. Several writings have drawn attention to the different aspects of faculty development, the one most prominent in terms of recent redefinition being a work entitled *Faculty Development in a Time of Retrenchment.*[10] The authors of this work, and several others discuss both the scope and necessity of FD, especially in times of stable or decreasing enrollments, and when many faculty members are destined to spend long periods of time, if not their entire careers, at one institution. In short, colleges must improve teaching and renew their faculties through methods other than urging professors to rededicate themselves to their profession, by providing stop-gap assistance in methodology, by readjusting content, or by offering merit pay for performance.[11]

There are any number of tenets and precepts for FD programs and just as many authors reiterating existing criteria and creating and examining new ones. One such example is an article by Bergquist and Phillips, which elaborates on precisely how to systematically develop, implement, and evaluate FD programs.[12] The authors propose that there are propositions basic to any examination or consideration of a viable faculty development program, and these propositions or criteria are as follows:

1. The process of teaching is one major role of college faculty members and must be considered by both the profession and administrators.

2. The process of teaching should be considered in its entirety since it frequently is not, by design, part of a college teacher's preparation.

3. The process of teaching should be a major consideration in areas of promotion and tenure.

4. The process of teaching should be given high priority in terms of internal grants and funding.

Faculty development, although in many ways similar to instructional development, is more oriented toward the development of the individual faculty members and their professional growth. Earlier in this chapter, the authors mentioned the considerable overlap between faculty and instructional development; there are also many areas of difference. When looking at faculty development, many authors and professors alike look toward such easily recognizable areas as research, continuing education, retrenchment, and professional and personal renewal. Yet, there are many other aspects of faculty development. Whether one subscribes to theories of growth, such as those put forward by Roger Gould and Daniel Levinson of Yale University, or whether one looks at a more contemporary work such as Gale Sheehy's *Passages*, most authorities recognize that there are many stages of human growth and development that clearly go beyond the bounds of any profession.

The hypothesis that adults develop through various stages in their lives, many of which are predictable, is not only interesting but worthy of both consideration and further research. The practical implications of such a hypothesis are many for faculty and developers, and those developers and college administrators need to be particularly cognizant of research in this area as programs are created and restructured.

SUMMARY

The premise that faculty development services to the university are necessary is hardly open to challenge; the location of these services is. Whether or not faculty development services are organizationally placed under the office of the vice president of academic affairs or within learning resources is certainly an open question. The most popular line and staff organization plans probably would locate faculty development services within or under the offices of the president, the vice president of academic affairs, or the offices of institutional research and development. The authors' rationale for presenting faculty development within learning resources rests on two premises.

First, when faculty and instructional development are viewed in the broadest sense, they are compatible enough to be offered from the same office. Second, since the differences between faculty and instructional development are often confused by administrators, faculty members, and media people, they need to be identified. Faculty development, a very necessary service in any college, may be located or housed under several administrative structures in an effective, efficient manner. One logical area for these services is learning resources.

Readers interested in a more in-depth discussion of faculty development are referred to Jerry Gaff's 1973 book *Toward Faculty Development*, where a contrast between faculty and instructional development is presented. It should be noted that when faculty development services reach the level where designated faculty developers are given the responsibility for faculty development councils, seminars, classes, etc., and when these development specialists offer courses in instructional/faculty developmental skills, the institution is certainly ready to consider faculty and instructional development as one. Also, at this time, the location and organization of faculty development centers, seminars and general organizations require thorough analysis as to their direction, their scope, and special needs.

NOTES

[1] J. R. Pfund, *Instructional Development in Perspective* (State University of New York, Oswego College of Arts and Sciences, 1975), ED 121272, p. 6.

[2] Ibid., p. 8.

[3] C. Robert Pace, *Evaluating Higher Education*, Topical Paper No. 1 (University of Arizona, Tucson College of Education, July 1976), ED 131737, pp. 2-4.

[4] Norman K. Henderson, *University Teaching* (Hong Kong: University Press, 1969), p. 9.

[5] Kenneth E. Eble, *Professors as Teachers* (San Francisco: Jossey-Bass, 1972), p. 104.

[6] Ibid., p. 111.

[7] Ohmer Milton and Edward J. Shoben, Jr., *Learning and the Professors* (Athens, OH: Ohio University Press, 1968), p. XVII.

[8] Eble, p. 111.

[9] Jerry G. Gaff, *Toward Faculty Renewal* (San Francisco: Joseey-Bass, 1975), p. 3.

[10] Group for Human Development in Higher Education, *Faculty Development in a Time of Retrenchment* (New Rochelle, NY: Change Magazine, 1974), pp. 19-26.

[11] Ibid., p. 17.

[12] William H. Bergquist and Steven R. Phillips, "Components of an Effective Faculty Development Program," *The Journal of Higher Education* 46 (March/April 1975): 177-211.

7

TECHNICAL SERVICES

The reader should note that in the organizational model in Chapter 3 (Figure 10, page 51) the authors placed the technical services unit in the division called Information and Resources. This is contrary to the generally accepted organizational patterns in existence in most academic libraries today, and it should not be construed to mean that the authors attach any less importance to the function of this unit than they do to those of the public services. It is, however, an effort to project technical services personnel, with inherent strengths in selection and organization of knowledge, into a more meaningful role in the academic process.

This chapter will address alternatives in organization that might provide more meaningful participation for the technical services personnel in the educational task. An examination of how the traditional unit with its various services might function in a learning resource center follows. General discussions of organization and personnel will illustrate how selection and acquisition, cataloging and classification, processing and handling, and some recent developments affect the LRC.

ORGANIZATION

The direction in which technical services as a unit has moved (and the general consensus appears that it has moved away from the mainstream of the academic community) makes it imperative that we take a hard look at its function. While the historical development of the technical services function parallels the history of libraries, its development as a separate unit within the library took place in the last half century.[1] In light of Helen Tuttle's research, it appears that a point may have been reached in the historical development of technical services where media administrators need to make a critical analysis of that unit's function. She stated:

> The isolation of the technical services in a separate division is a function of size . . . first a separate unit is established to handle cataloging, then one for acquisitions, later serials, and finally, all of them together as a separate division with its specialist head. . . . Academic and

research libraries have tended to dominate change and codification in this area of library work, as much in 1876 as in 1976.[2]

The detrimental effect of such isolation is evident in both the library itself and in the academic community. Ultimately, it is the user who suffers the loss of expertise that technical services personnel can provide. This has been adequately pointed out by Doralyn Hickey and Tuttle respectively:

> . . . library services are designed to move materials through the system and on to storage shelves, there to be interpreted by a group of people who have little or nothing to do with the procedures which put materials into storage.[3]

> It has been said that as the specialists took over the technical services, the user was lost to view. . . . Harrassed by floods of materials . . . and arrearages simultaneously, the technical services staff may indeed lose track of the ultimate customer, an oversight which must receive more attention in the future.[4]

But simply to make a statement that all technical services personnel are removed from the mainstream of academic life is to make a generalization unfair to those institutions that have worked at projecting all library personnel into their respective academic roles. Some institutions are small enough so that separate units have not yet developed, while others are large enough to have subject specialists breaking out of their isolation. Too few have transcended the isolation, however, and Tuttle's advice about academic leadership in this area is timely and directive.

The director of the LRC has options in placing the technical services unit into the organizational framework or in devising an organizational pattern that ignores the unit and places these services into other subdivisions. The final decisions, however, are governed by the expectations held of that unit, regardless of where it is placed. On the one hand, if the unit is working in isolation, it matters little where it is placed in the structure of learning resources. In fact, other technical services dealing with commercially and locally produced instructional materials could also be channelled into this unit in order to centralize similar functions. On the other hand, however, leaders in instructional development and design have long realized the value of keeping production specialists closely involved while working with faculty, for it reduces the fear of having to guard against their isolation from the instructional process. This practice is an important one to keep in mind as organizations are established.

Hickey, in her work on a revised relationship between public and technical services, does a succinct analysis of what has been tried in various institutions and has some projections as to what might be tried. In adapting some Ralph Shaw philosophy to the problem, she indicates that "It appears reasonably clear that the naiveté of the user's approach to the library demands from the library staff a group of services which transcends the division between public and technical functions."[5] LRC directors who do not acquaint themselves with her work are at a disadvantage. One of her basic premises can be easily aligned to what generally happens in the instructional technology unit, and the authors encourage exploration of such direction in reorganization. She made the following observation:

A fairly obvious solution to such a dilemma is to reorient the library's systems around the concept of direct and effective service to the clientele. What currently exists is an orientation toward indirect service to the clientele. If any direct service is involved, it is apparently aimed at the preservation and storage of materials rather than the solution of user's problems.[6]

Perhaps the orientation can be achieved more easily through a restructuring of the LRC organization, and certainly the development of newer and better technology will force an examination of existing structures. For that very reason, the authors have chosen to look at the various ways that technical services can fit into an organizational pattern. It will serve to further detail the rationale as to why the more moderate organizational structure shown in Figure 10 was presented as a working model.

The range of models depicted here runs from one of isolation to one of complete integration. Figure 12 is the more commonplace situation in which the technical services are a fairly isolated unit.

Figure 12

Technical Services Isolated in the LRC

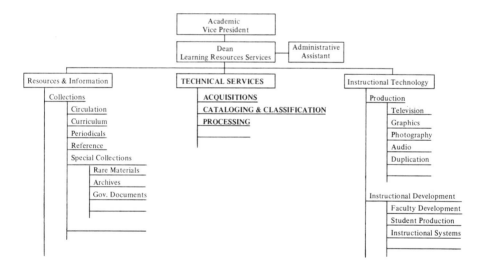

The major advantage of placing the technical services into an organizational structure in such a manner is immediately obvious: it provides for a very high degree of specialization, especially as the organization grows larger. While providing for a very efficient unit in bringing like functions together, it does have the disadvantage of isolating persons well-versed in materials from the user.

The placement of the technical services unit into the organizational structure shown in Figure 13, as integral parts of both the major service units, can bring the personnel of the technical service units into a more meaningful relationship with the personnel of the parent units. It may help to break the isolation, but it does perhaps have the disadvantage of requiring technical expertise in two separate areas. It is, however, a movement toward the integration of technical services into public services units.

Figure 13

Technical Services Integrated in the LRC

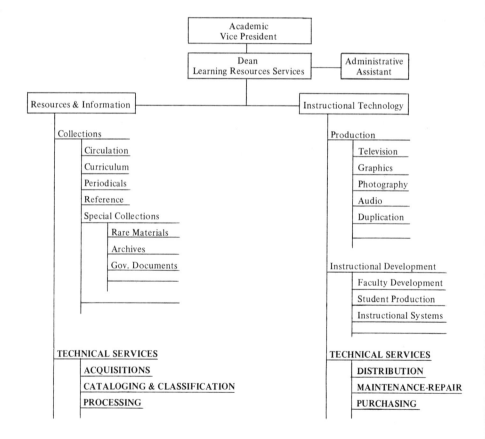

Figure 13 shows technical services as a part of both the major divisions, and as such, each unit of the major division is responsible for the functions of the technical services commonly associated with that division. In this way, acquisition of materials for information and services (books, films, documents, etc.) will be provided by the acquisitions unit within that unit; and the cataloging and processing of those same materials will be handled there likewise. Equipment, materials and supplies for instructional services, etc., will be acquired and processed by the technical services unit within the instructional technology unit.

If the professional aspects of technical services (i.e., cataloging, selection of materials, etc.) are integrated into the various components of the major divisions, then a technical *processing* unit could be established that would handle the technical responsibilities (placing of orders, receiving, processing, etc.) for both divisions. This would dictate very definitive job descriptions that clearly delineate the responsibilities of each subdivision; this ensures that the professional aspects are carried out both prior to the assignment of a specific responsibility to the technical processing unit and upon the return of the processed materials to the originating unit. The placement of a technical processing unit into an organizational structure is shown in Figure 14.

Figure 14
Centralized Technical Processing Unit in the LRC

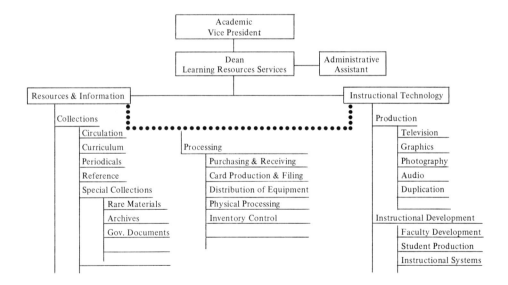

As indicated in Figure 14, the professional personnel in such an organization are freed to work with clientele simply because their basic responsibility rests in a position that requires constant communication with the public. It has the additional advantage of putting similar technical *processing* functions into one unit, with only a certain amount of professional supervision required. The basic responsibility of working with materials from their selection to their dissemination remains with the professionals.

The organizational pattern shown in Figure 15 serves the same purpose for technical *processing* that Figure 13 (page 116) did for technical services. It makes provision for each major division to have its own technical processing unit, yet it keeps people in those units responsible for professional technical services within the major subdivisions. This tends to keep professional personnel working more closely with clients even though a certain proportion of their work will be directed toward what are normally technical service responsibilities. Figure 15 represents the kind of organizational structure wherein professional technical responsibilities are integrated into the whole organization.

Figure 15
Technical Processing Dispersed in the LRC

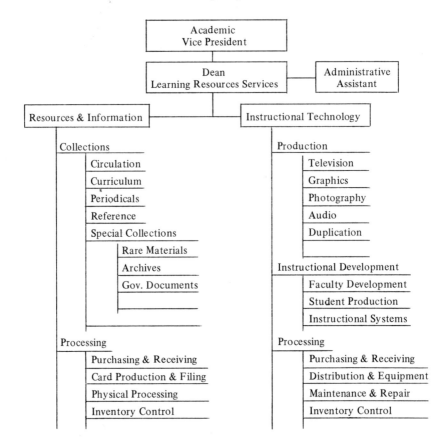

The advantages of integrating technical services into public services units are obviously related to deployment of personnel into a more meaningful role because of the expertise gained in handling materials. It does not separate those personnel from the user, but its application may be more than the new LRC may want to take on in its beginning stages. For that reason, the reader is referred back to Figure 10 (page 51) in Chapter three, the Suggested LRC Organizational Chart developed by the authors.

The authors' model, a combination of the organizational patterns presented in Figures 13 and 15, provides a technical services subdivision for resources and information and an integrated technical processing unit for instructional technology services. It indicates, at best, a movement from isolation (Figure 12, page 115), which the authors feel to be least desirable, to complete integration (Figure 15), which will enable the institution to take utmost advantage of the professional abilities of its members who work in public service roles.

PERSONNEL

The integration of technical services personnel into the public services units, as shown in Figure 10, might at first glance seem to be a traditional technical services unit. It should be noted, however, that the organization is directly related not only to how administrators see the function of that unit but also to how the personnel within that unit see their own roles. Only a determined effort to bring professional personnel into a service-oriented role will produce the desired results, for within the organization, personnel will have the latitude to determine the direction of their participation. They can function in isolation or as the subject specialists described by Eldred Smith in his essay on subject specialists in the academic research library. Smith readily admits that the subject specialist has not yet appeared in great numbers, but that many institutions (especially the larger ones) have brought them into both branch and main libraries. He also admits to the existence in libraries of subject specialists (as opposed to generalists) for quite some time, but he points out that these have, for the most part, "remained primarily housekeepers, running their units with more or less efficiency—sometimes with considerable efficiency—but at a minimal service level."[7]

Somewhere between the generalist and the subject specialist lies the media person described by Evert Volkersz in his work on collegial involvement. He stated:

> In breaking out of the hierarchical structure librarians have renewed the dialogue while challenging the authoritarian nature of academic library life. Collegial involvement encourages individual growth and development in concert with other faculty. This interdependence contrasts with the traditional relationship, in which most librarians neither shared responsibility for, nor participated in, making the crucial decisions shaping their contributions to teaching research, collection development, and community involvement.[8]

It is only with this kind of collegiality that we will finally realize the full potential of the technical services personnel; and as more networking and automation reduces the amount of professional staff necessary, the unit can be reduced to a technical processing section for many of its functions. Professional staff can then be deployed into other units for more effective professional work in both supervisory and service positions. Volkersz placed this in perspective:

> Close analysis of these activities may suggest the need for organizational restructuring of the library, freeing faculty with academic responsibilities from administrative burdens, and streamlining the activities of production-oriented departments. . . . Automation of technical processes and bibliographic data bases seriously challenges librarians now engaged in marginal professional duties, and may also lead to reassignment of experienced librarians.[9]

From this point of view, it is quite conceivable that technical processing units can be formed wherein professional work is limited to supervision; professional personnel would then join the mainstream of the educational process, either through work with students or faculty. Perhaps the organization as a whole remains within the purview of the administrator who is not limited in his imagination and has not developed a hide-bound tradition that limits the basic purpose of the learning resources program. In the final analysis, the judicious placement of personnel who have the expertise commonly associated with technical services can be justified on the more solid tradition of service to clientele. Only then will the words of people like Hickey become a reality: "If the basic philosophy of librarianship is to match materials with the needs of people, then it seems clear that a more client-oriented structure of library service is required."[10]

ACQUISITIONS

It is difficult to speak about acquisitions without making additional comments about selection. While selection, from the basis of collections development, was to some degree covered in Chapter four, little was said about methodology. In effect, the LRC differs little from the traditional library in selection and acquisition except in the scope of its involvement in the selection of materials in all formats. The LRC is based on the concept of learning alternatives and the development of a base of alternative ideas. The selection of materials in all formats must be built upon a policy that provides for a comprehensive collection.

The administration of selection has usually been carried out by the acquisitions section of technical services, but selection itself has generally involved and must continue to involve students, faculty, and library personnel. Guy Lyle has quite succinctly phrased what the organization of book (in the generic sense) selection must be:

> The organization of book selection in most college libraries operates under a system of departmental allocations, but with ample flexibility in the program for the library staff to be an active force. The purpose of such organization is to emphasize a coordinated library-faculty effort to select the best of the current output, to provide a high degree of immediate availability in those subjects which are taught in

the college curriculum, and to attempt to strengthen the collection by filling in the lacunae.[11]

That is indeed an excellent guide for the LRC to use in establishing its selection policies, and on the surface it appears to be an easy solution to the problem of selection and acquisition of materials in other than the printed form. To extend the principles of book selection to other materials and to supplement that procedure with consideration of their production and technical qualities is what selection of those materials is all about. Carter, Bonk, and Magrill have pointed out, however, that the major problems involved in nonbook selection are actually administrative, and that too often selection problems are avoided altogether because of anticipated difficulty in handling the materials.[12]

Carter, Bonk, and Magrill's work is certainly as comprehensive and as classic a work as exists in the selection of print materials, and they have attempted to provide some guidelines for the selection of other materials as well. By their own admission, however, the work does not make adequate provision for the guidelines and methodology necessary to select and acquire materials other than print. They stated:

> The enlarged acquisition of such materials has brought with it an increased concern with problems of selecting the material, sources of information about and methods of acquisitions of the various types, and problems of handling the non-book forms once they are acquired. This field is so extensive that full treatment of the problem in all its aspects would require a separate volume.[13]

Nonprint Media in the Academic Library, a 1975 work edited by Pearce Grove and published under the auspices of the Audiovisual Committee of the Association of College and Research Libraries, provides hope for help in the nonprint areas; but rapid technological advances dictate the need for updating, despite its recency.[14] The appearance of more and more selection tools since publication of the Grove work also has helped library personnel to wade through the materials flooding the market. The authors suggest that comprehensive works like those by Carter, Bonk, and Magrill and by Grove, along with updated materials, be used to guide library personnel in the selection and acquisition of materials for the LRC. However, a brief summary of guiding principles for learning resources follows, and these should form the foundation for both selection and acquisition.

Personnel in Acquisitions

Although all members of the academic community must be involved, learning resources personnel assume ultimate responsibility for good collection development. Coordination of selection and acquisitions should be provided by the professional person in charge of acquisitions. Special strengths of college faculty should be solicited in the selection of items for all collections, but they should be especially involved in the selection of expensive items through preview. For this reason, selection tools, bibliographies, sales brochures, professional journals, and any other selection sources should be made available to departmental members. Student requests should be solicited and departmental allocations should be made. Learning resources staff members should select materials both to support their particular collections (e.g., reference, periodicals, etc.) and to support particular subject specialities, thereby insuring the development of a balanced collection.

Selection Policies and Procedures

A definitive, written selection policy should form the basis for the selection of materials if collections are to be developed in a directed, well-organized manner. Of definite help in developing such a policy is the work entitled "Guidelines for the Formulation of Collection Development Policies," published by ALA and completed by the Collection Development Committee, Resource Section, Resource and Technical Services Division. (A copy of that work is included herein as Appendix A.) Duplication should be avoided whenever possible and networking must be considered in the acquisition of expensive items. Problem areas—such as periodicals, audio materials, video materials, etc.—must have clearly defined policies to provide for judicious use of funds and to avoid copyright violations. Materials should be selected in support of the curriculum and in relation to holdings. The type of institution and its mission will dictate the depth of research materials.

All materials should be selected through the use of professionally accepted selection tools, through preview or through recommendations of professionally recognized people. All materials scheduled for preview should be channeled through acquisitions; and departments and LRC personnel should be involved in previewing.

Budget allocations should be made to colleges, schools, and/or departments, and while some form of cost accounting is desirable, it may not always be feasible. Selections should be monitored only so that imbalances of materials, both in subject matter and in format, may be avoided, as the LRC staff maintains its responsibility to develop a well-rounded, useful collection of materials.

Acquisition of Materials and Equipment

Perhaps the most succinct, useful work to appear in the literature of technical services on "how to" procedures is that of Warren Hicks and Alma Tillin. They have characterized the acquisitions procedure as consisting of four basic functions: searching, ordering, accounting, and receiving; and the flow chart they have developed is as comprehensive as an LRC dean might envision in establishing routines for acquisitions.[15] The authors recommend it highly as a model.

While administration of equipment was covered in instructional technical services, some facets of the acquisition function could easily be carried out within the acquisitions unit. Acquisition of equipment must be based on need. That need is expressed both through the depth and scope of materials requiring special equipment and through use. Centralizing or decentralizing of equipment would also have a bearing on the amount of equipment necessary to meet academic needs. The selection of equipment is also not limited to any one person, nor is it subject to the wishes of individuals or single departments. While individuals or departments may express needs, the acquisition of equipment should be handled by those persons who best know the specifications most desirable for the institution. It is conceivable, and perhaps feasible, that the acquisition of equipment be handled by the acquisitions section. The expertise of that department in working with the business office, in working with jobbers and vendors, and in maintaining the necessary accounting will lead to more efficiency in the purchasing procedure. Recommendations for purchase should come from those who possess expertise in the use of equipment—from personnel in production who work daily with a multitude of equipment, from personnel in periodicals who work with microform readers, from television personnel who work daily with that equipment, etc. Salesmen who visit the academic campus should be encouraged to spend time in these various areas working with the people who use the equipment in their daily work. Recommendations should then be made to acquisitions, where the mechanical procedures of ordering and purchasing are carried out.

CATALOGING AND CLASSIFICATION

Physical access to materials is maintained through a good system of bibliographic control and bibliographic access. Generally, this is accomplished through production of an index or catalog, all or parts of which can be produced locally or purchased in their entirety. Whether this index or catalog provides data through the traditional method of searching or through some automated means, it remains the key to the identification of materials and to their subsequent retrieval for use. For most libraries or LRCs, the key to the use of the collection and to the retrieval of information is the card catalog, a complex compendium of subject cataloging, descriptive cataloging, and classification information.

It is almost paradoxical that the persons who produce and understand fully this intricate retrieval system are also the most often misunderstood and maligned members of the learning resource staff. Opinions as to the productivity, the idiosyncracies, and the value of catalogers, and hence their work, span the range of possible positive and negative reactions. Whatever the status of the catalog department or of the catalogers themselves, though, two factors seem to remain constant— expertise in cataloging and classification underlies the retrieval of materials, and the cataloging field itself is in a constant state of flux despite its rigid self-imposed standards.

In chronicling the history of cataloging, Tuttle has taken us from Cutter to computer, but in so doing, she notes that the difficulty in making change has been underscored by a reluctance to change. Speaking of computers, she makes an indirect conclusion that characterizes the cataloging field today:

There is still a long, fascinating trail to travel. Full exploitation of computers has been handicapped by our thinking in traditional terms. Networking tends to be thought of as an extension of present services rather than rethought as a new concept with new potential. The fact that new machines impose new conditions on their users is another reason why the traditional conceptions must be rethought.[16]

Too many catalogers see the status quo as the retention of standards, and they are prone to point out that "Catalogers have had trouble explaining their work to other librarians who have a different training and experience."[17] The cataloging department, no matter how large or how small, cannot function in a situation that reflects a reluctance to change on the one hand and the implication of technological developments on the other.

In formulating a philosophical base for the process of document retrieval, as opposed to information retrieval, the thoughts of renowned scholar Jesse Shera are appropriate; speaking to the "librarian-documentalist," he stated:

> We have already seen that machines alone, of and by themselves, will not solve our problems; imagination and intelligence are essential to their fullest utilization. This means that the future librarian must be a specialist in the discipline of bibliographic organization. Over and above a sound general education he must be thoroughly informed regarding the basic principles and techniques of librarianship; he must know the literature of some specific subject field or group of related subject fields; and above all he must comprehend the uses to which the literature of these fields is put.[18]

This has implications for change in the role of both the cataloger and other personnel in the resource center, and as LRC personnel move more toward the automation of special aspects of librarianship, Shera's thoughts on automation should be kept foremost:

> The real purpose of library automation is to accomplish with ease and efficiency those tasks which existing library techniques and devices (i.e., the card catalogs, the bibliographies, the indices) either cannot now do or can do only with the greatest difficulty and inconvenience.[19]

The administrator of the LRC, who is ultimately responsible for the efficiency and effectiveness of both the cataloger and the cataloging process, must not be blinded by traditional methodology; nor can the administrator be averse to upholding standards that result in a catalog that contains the entries necessary to make documents and information retrieval easy, effective, and economical. If this means reorganization to make more effective use of personnel, an option made possible through commercial cataloging, automation, or some other process, then within the LRC, catalogers may take a more meaningful role in the academic life of the community they serve. In this context, personnel utilization, along with procedures and policies of the cataloging and classification process, are discussed.

Personnel Utilization in Cataloging and Classification

The art of cataloging and classification is work that can not be relegated to the paraprofessional or clerical worker, but many procedures within the purview of the cataloging unit can. Sometimes procedures are not clear cut, and therein lies the problem most often faced by the administrator who chooses to institute procedures that, in the eyes of many catalogers, tend to demean the importance of their work or to lower standards. This problem can be alleviated by careful examination of two related personnel activities. The first pertains to the writing of clear, definitive job descriptions and is fairly easy to accomplish; the second pertains to attitudes and takes more patience, time, and direction.

Clearly defined parameters for professional job responsibilities provide assurance that the professional cataloger will not become bogged down with routine duties. Professional time may already be limited to processing an ever-increasing abundance of materials needing classification and cataloging. Indeed, the huge backlog of materials in many cataloging departments can be attributed in part to catalogers who choose or are forced to perform duties that could more easily and beneficially be the responsibility of a clerical or paraprofessional worker.

An even greater stumbling block to streamlining the cataloging unit is an unwillingness on the part of too many catalogers to accept the integrity of the cataloging and classification performed elsewhere. An attitudinal change becomes a prerequisite to any system of networking in technical services, to the acceptance of cataloging by the Library of Congress, and to the purchase of preprocessed materials.

Attitudinal changes are difficult to initiate and sustain since they can shake the secure foundation of maintaining the cataloging status quo. Only when change is accompanied by assurances that it will not be followed by a loss of standards or be a threat to job security can much be accomplished. In many instances, some well-prepared data on cost-benefit management as opposed to the value of the purist point of view may be the beginning of attitudinal change; in others, some firm administrative decisions, based on research and investigation, may be the only answer to a problem that simply cannot be resolved in any other way.

Basic to all policy development is the full utilization of clerical, paraprofessional, and technical personnel. Ultimately, this provides the time necessary for professionals to pursue at academic and professional levels the challenges of technological advances. Only through intense study, constant evaluation and reevaluation, and experience at the local level can policies become the driving force behind successful procedures.

Cataloging and Classification Procedures and Policies

The main responsibility of the cataloging and classification unit has been and continues to be the preparation and maintenance of the bibliographic data base used in retrieval and access. Other work, such as de-acquisition and inventorying, are also assigned to that unit within most library organizations. It would be unfortunate, however, if the LRC director today were not to heed the words of Berrisford when he analyzed the year's work for 1976: "The communication and display of bibliographic data are being affected by new technologies, and the traditional card catalog is being challenged effectively."[20]

Policies and procedures are destined to be affected by meaningful change within the field, and Berrisford pointed out that change in cataloging and classification was both constant and continuing. Not only does he indicate that more changes are to come, but he also states that much of the change revolves around automation. Constant monitoring of technological advances, with a resulting application of new developments when human and financial resources permit, is therefore essential in procedures and policy development.[21]

Organization of work in cataloging will vary with its basic responsibilities to the LRC. Lyle listed four basic methods of dividing work within the cataloging unit: by function, by subject, by language, and by type of materials.[22] These remain workable alternatives, but the amount of original cataloging and classification necessary will undoubtedly be the biggest factor in determining both the number of personnel and their work responsibilities.

Hicks and Tillin have divided the cataloging process into four major procedures: description, analysis, classification, and catalog production. The flow chart developed by them is an analysis of "work division and the sequence of its performance" in carrying through these procedures.[23] It would be redundant if the authors were to reconstruct such a comprehensive flow chart with its accompanying description of the cataloging and classification procedures. On the other hand, they would be remiss were they not to refer to its existence as an exemplary guide to the development of cataloging and classification procedures. Each institution, within the confines of its own goals and objectives, must make its own adaptations to such a master plan.

The degree of efficiency and the professionalism with which the cataloging and classification unit carries out its work will be closely related to well-developed policies. Development of policies and a guidelines handbook will not only solidify operational procedures, but it will also insure continuity within a rapidly changing and developing field. While the policies of this unit within the LRC are not any more permissive in nature than those in the traditional library, it is important to note that some will need to be viewed in an expanded role.

Policies within cataloging and classification need to reflect the realization that the recording of knowledge transcends the written word. This makes it imperative that the LRC provide access to all formats of materials through bibliographic control; thus, it requires an unbiased view toward materials from the professional people working in the unit. It requires, first and foremost, uniform cataloging and classification; and with the many options available for the various formats, it is not only essential that this be done, but also that it be done in some systematized manner within the framework of well-developed policies.

The integrity of cataloging and classification policies used in the development of the tools used in bibliographic accessibility (i.e., card catalog, book catalog, indexes, etc.) comes only from a dependence upon the guidelines set forth in commonly accepted works in the field. Standard works must serve as guides, while a work as extensive in the nonprint area as that of Grove helps to fill voids. A list of basic cataloging and classification tools useful to the LRC includes the following:

American Library Association. *ALA Rules for Filing Catalog Cards.* 2nd ed. Chicago: ALA, 1949.

American Library Association, et al. *Anglo-American Cataloging Rules*, North American Text. Chicago: ALA, 1967. (Reissued with supplement, 1970).

Dewey, Melvil. *Dewey Classification and Relative Index.* Lake Placid, NY: Forest Press Division, Lake Placid Education Foundation, 1971. 3v.

National Union Catalog. London: Mansell, 1968- .

U.S. Library of Congress. *The National Union Catalog.* Washington: Government Printing Office, 1956- . (Title varies).

U.S. Library of Congress, Processing Department, Catalog Publication Division. *Films and Other Materials for Projection, 1973-* . Washington: Library of Congress, 1974- .

U.S. Library of Congress, Processing Department, Catalog Publication Division. *Music: Books on Music and Sound Recordings, 1973-* . Washington: Library of Congress, 1974- .

U.S. Library of Congress, Processing Department, Subject Cataloging Division. *Classification Schedules.* Washington: Government Printing Office, date varies. 3v.

U.S. Library of Congress, Processing Department, Subject Cataloging Division. *Library of Congress Subject Headings.* 8th ed. Washington: Government Printing Office, 1975.

* * *

The following is an example of an OCLC on-line manual:

PALINET and Union Library Catalogue of Pennsylvania. *Manual for Operation of the OCLC 100 Terminal and the OCLC System.* Philadelphia: PALINET, 1976.

* * *

The following MARC format manuals should be included:

U.S. Library of Congress. MARC Development Office. *Books: A MARC Format.* 5th ed. Washington: Library of Congress, 1972.

U.S. Library of Congress. MARC Development Office. *Books: A MARC Format. Addenda.* Washington: Library of Congress, 1972-

U.S. Library of Congress. MARC Development Office. *Music: A MARC Format.* Washington: Library of Congress, undated.

U.S. Library of Congress. MARC Development Office. *Serials: A MARC Format.* 2nd ed. Washington: Library of Congress, 1974.

U.S. Library of Congress. MARC Development Office. *Films: A MARC Format.* Washington: Library of Congress, undated.

U.S. Library of Congress. MARC Development Office. *MARC Serials Editing Guide.* CONSER ed. Washington: Library of Congress, 1975.

* * *

Dependence upon professionally developed tools and an adherence to well-defined standards are essential, but just as critical is a common sense approach in application. This is especially true at a time when there is a proliferation of materials during a period of austerity budgeting and spending. A certain amount of flexibility must be built into cataloging and classification policies since both rapid professional changes and adaptation to local goals and objectives will dictate change.

The physical processing of materials can precede, in part, the classification and cataloging thereof. The next section will attempt to deal from a policy standpoint with that aspect of work in the LRC.

TECHNICAL PROCESSING AND HANDLING

Some general guidelines and policies on technical processing and the handling of materials and equipment, even though these functions might be carried out in different units, can provide a framework of continuity within the LRC. Of central importance is the fact that tasks within technical processing be accomplished in an expedient manner by nonprofessional personnel in various levels of preparation. With the exception of some help in maintenance and repair, which will require technical expertise from personnel trained in electronics or mechanics, the amount of professional help required will be primarily supervisory. Whenever feasible, trained personnel (i.e., library technicians, paraprofessionals, etc.) should be employed to provide efficiency and a high level of performance in work that may require particular skills.

Three procedures in the technical processing and handling should be considered mandatory before materials and equipment are allowed to circulate among LRC clientele or staff. All of these can easily be performed in the receiving unit, and all should be completed as soon after arrival as possible: 1) checking items against invoices to insure receipt of correct items; 2) checking for obvious imperfections in expensive items and for performance in equipment; and 3) placing of ownership identification on the item. Two guidelines should be adopted with respect to these procedures—the checks for imperfections and operations should be done only if they prove to be cost effective, and the placement of ownership markings should reflect a feeling for the aesthetic.

Once materials have been classified and cataloged, technical processing should be completed as soon as possible to provide clientele access to them. No attempt will be made here at any in-depth treatise on the processing of materials, for the range of formats makes it difficult to set rigid standards. What is important is the establishment of routines that will move materials quickly and efficiently through the processing area. Some experimentation will undoubtedly be necessary in light of circulation problems caused by varying shapes and sizes of both materials and containers. Much time can also be saved in the technical processing of materials by using available mechanical devices and equipment designed to reduce the amount of manual labor involved in simple procedures. The supervisor of technical processing must be constantly alert to the development of labor-saving devices and equipment available within the processing field.

Many processes that are considered technical follow the actual physical processing of materials and equipment, and many of these functions cut across unit lines. While direct responsibility for some of these functions does not fall immediately within the confines of technical services, some aspects of the work involved do lie there, and the responsibility for execution, therefore, demands concrete policies. These functions will be considered in light of current practices and philosophical concepts.

Current Practices Affecting Technical Processing Services

Many practices within libraries today can no longer be termed "futures." The fact that they are indeed taking place makes it essential that LRC personnel be both aware of them and take them into consideration in planning. In his book entitled *Toward a Theory of Librarianship*, Robert Taylor spoke to change:

> It is neither daring nor unconventional—in fact it is rather banal—to assert that libraries have changed, are changing, and will change. The point is that most such assertions stop when this has been said, except for those flights of fancy that tell us what the library will be like some time in the future. . . .
>
> This paper, then, is an exploration of the kinds of questions we should ask and of the options open or closed to the profession as the institutional base changes. We cannot expect solid answers, for at present there are too many undefined, economic, educational, and cultural variables for any high degree of confidence. Our problem, then, becomes one of defining the pertinent questions, and of formulating the framework of those questions and of the kinds of answers we can anticipate; what we know with reasonable assurance and what we do not know, because this is the only basis upon which we can plan future libraries *and* present education.[24]

It is from that kind of framework that the LRC personnel, and those in technical services specifically, need to view some of the newer practices in libraries today.

Automation, Mechanization, and Computer Applications

While there are those who differentiate among the three terms—and technically they are correct—the automation of library routines and practices revolves around the use of machines and computers. In effect, the definitions are not important; rather, the process is. It is extremely important to keep in mind the admonition of Robert Taylor that "automation itself is not a change, because it operates within the conventional framework of library processes. It is merely a refinement of current practices."[25]

It is important that LRC personnel realize that the turn to automation and the use of machines and computers begin with an analysis of needs at the local level. Many routine tasks lend themselves to automation, and the majority of these fall within the realm of technical services, even though the last few years have seen considerable expansion into other areas. Among those most easily automated are serials management, out-of-print list development, inventory control, circulation control, acquisitions processing, business procedures, catalog card reproduction, and book catalog development. Whatever application is contemplated, an excellent guideline is that proposed by Rogers and Weber, wherein they look at need, justification, system design, time and cost, and staff implications.[26]

The LRC today must be cognizant of automation and its implications, and care must be taken in staff development to insure inclusion of expertise in mechanization and computer application. It is highly recommended that the LRC director assign responsibility for automation, mechanization, and computer application to a single staff member. It could well become that staff member's responsibility, in turn, to analyze, recommend, and design in conjunction with other staff members and the computer center, the implementation of feasible application.

Consortiums and Library Networks

There appears to be little consistency in term definition within the entire field of library cooperation. Pointing out this lack of generally agreed upon definitions, J. Michael Bruer reported:

> The situation with respect to networking and resource sharing is becoming so complex, and conditions are changing so rapidly, that there is danger of everyone going off in separate directions with increasing loss of communication. . . . Confusion over definitions and terminology is often symptomatic of deeper issues and is to be expected in the early stages of grappling with large and complex problems. . . .[27]

These factors should not deter the LRC director from examining participation in any type of resource sharing or networking. In light of communication difficulties resulting from a lack of cogent definitions, perhaps the director needs to approach the problem by examining participation at two levels—the immediate and the more far-reaching.

The immediate, for practical purposes, should be one that involves a number of institutions that decide on resource sharing because of proximity or geographical boundaries. An example of such an immediate resource sharing consortium is the one in the metropolitan Minneapolis-St. Paul area entitled Cooperating Libraries in Consortium (CLIC). Incorporated in 1969, it now has seven private college libraries and one reference library as members. Its basic purpose continues to be resource sharing through interlibrary loan, and as of September 1977, its data base included some 260,000 items. The complete retrospective data base is expected to be completed in 1978, and the consortium is presently working on developing a machine-readable catalog. It should be noted that while CLIC's present direction is toward user service, it still vitally affects technical services.

An example of the more far-reaching network system is the Ohio College Library Center (OCLC), started as a state project and now developed nationally. A look at that prototype should present the options available through networking today, with an eye toward what may be available in the future. Begun in 1967 as an attempt to offer Ohio's academic libraries on-line batch processing catalog service, OCLC soon expanded to include other networks as well. With an expanding data base of catalog records, it can be described as a system that has on-line shared, cooperative cataloging for an increasing number of libraries. Barbara

Markuson's 1976 report in *Library Technology Reports* is well worth reading. Her comprehensive report on why libraries join networks, how transitions to on-line operations have been handled, how staffs have reacted to the use of terminals, and how on-line operations have affected cost, staffing, production, and workflow are essential to any organization contemplating joining on-line networks. Especially valuable is her summary of "OCLC Services by Operational Status" with its accompanying explanation.[28] Data taken from her work appear in Figure 16.

Figure 16
OCLC Services by Operational Status

I. Operational Services

    A.   Data base searching for monographs and serials
    B.   Monograph and serials cataloging from records in data base
    C.   Original cataloging for monographs and serials
    D.   Reclassification and conversion projects
    E.   Automatic formatting of spine and book labels
    F.   Production of catalog cards for monographs
    G.   Production of accessions lists
    H.   Production of archive tapes from local input
    I.   Update of local records input to data base

II. In Transition to Operational Status

    A.   Serials Check-In

III. Services Currently under Development or Study

    A.   Cataloging and card production for non-book formats and serials
    B.   Local holdings records for monographs
    C.   Acquisitions Control (called Technical Processing by OCLC)
    D.   Interlibrary Loan
    E.   Subject access to OCLC data base
    F.   Information retrieval from non-OCLC data bases
    G.   Serials claiming and binding control

IV. Services Included in Long-Range Plans

    A.   On-Line Catalog with Authority Files
    B.   Circulation Control System

Preliminary decisions on how technical services will be affected by networking can be made from studies such as the one by Markuson and pilot projects initiated to test its implications. Perhaps the most comprehensive work on cooperative programs has been that by Weber;[29] and although in his article he laments, and rightly so, the lack of good studies on cooperation, the bibliography is noteworthy. He points out the significance of on-line cataloging and stated that "adoption of sophisticated on-line computer-based programs may well be by far the most significant change ever achieved in library operations."[30]

Divided Catalog

Differences of opinion continue to exist as to whether to divide the card catalog. While libraries of all sizes have in selected cases divided their catalogs, the decision to do so has usually been based on whether or not the present card catalog was functional or not. Agnes Grady, in her work on divided catalogs, provided not only a selected bibliography but also some keen insights into the methods of dividing, the reasons for dividing, an analysis of use studies, and a look at studies of divided catalogs and accounts of division.[31] She concluded by saying: "A divided catalog is neither a last resort nor the ultimate in catalogs, but it may be the one most suitable for some individual libraries."[32] In the preface to her article, Grady noted that perhaps "formal instruction in bibliographic tools" might be more effective than a divided catalog.[33] The LRC that makes a decision based on a thorough study of catalog use to divide its catalog might well consider the methodology suggested by Donald Foster in his *Managing the Catalog Department*.[34]

Microforms and Microfilming

Developments in microform and microfilming bear watching in view of how they will affect LRC functions. While in-house or regional cooperation in microfilming must be carefully researched in light of cost effectiveness, some consideration should be given as well to user accessibility to materials that otherwise might be difficult to circulate.

There is a current trend toward better catalog access, and many institutions, either privately or commercially, have placed their card catalogs on microform. Combined with a computer catalog, this method—known as computer output microfilm (COM)—may well result in the demise of the card catalog per se. Certainly this type of catalog will affect the function and direction of technical services.

Reclassification

The LRC collection classified by the Dewey scheme may well present its administration with a dilemma as to whether or not to reclassify. This may be especially true when the LC classification system is presented as offering easier access to a national data bank and to on-line cataloging. The ultimate test is the answer to the fundamental question of which system best meets the needs of the LRC's clientele.

Should the LRC staff decide that it might be advantageous and cost-effective to reclassify, and that it might be in the best interests of the user, then a procedure recommended by Rogers and Weber is worth noting. When they spoke to staff participation in decision making, they reaffirmed the authors' personal experiences with such a venture:

> The change from the Dewey Decimal to the L.C. classification is a problem that should be studied and discussed extensively at the staff level before a definite decision is reached. The director . . . will weigh the disruptive effect that such a decision will have on established routines and the complexity of the solution: Should there be complete reclassification of the entire collection? should there be partial reclassification of very active branch or main reference collections or of serial sets? should the new classification be applied only to new acquisitions or to publications after 1970 except in literature? how will users be affected? what are the cost implications? what has been the experience of other libraries? what is the relationship of such a course to automation? how would partial reclassification affect deployment of collections and general space needs? how will the individual cataloger be affected? By the time these issues are discussed and clarified, the faculty may be enthusiastic about the prospect of adopting a new classification and the staff may have found effective ways for an immediate change.[35]

Once such staff commitment has been solicited and gained, the work of reclassification, except for planning and supervision, is basically clerical. A certain amount of training combined with well-established procedures, all based on both short- and long-range goals, will prove effective.

Deselection

Lyle, while admitting that weeding involves a selection process, does not support the idea that weeding a collection counted as book selection.[36] Barbara Rice, on the other hand, uses the word "deselection" and includes not only weeding but also "a review of materials being received on standing order or blanket order."[37] Gore's "zero-growth" concept referred to previously in this work includes an extensive weeding program to maintain a collection static in size. Whatever terms are used, and whatever philosophies are promulgated with respect to removing some materials from the collection, it becomes quite apparent that deselection must be part of every selection policy as evidenced by its inclusion in works on collection development.

It is not the purpose here to set forth criteria for a deselection policy, for most administrative manuals contain such information. Nor is there an attempt to promote the role of technical services in making decisions about deselection. Rather, the concerns of technical services in deselection can be summarized in the withdrawal function. Rice notes that "a program for the identification of weeded titles must be developed with this unit, and the time needed to revise or delete records must be integrated with other technical services activities."[38] Changing records, therefore, becomes part of the responsibility of technical services in maintaining a useful, accurate catalog; and a clearly defined procedure, meticulously followed and carefully supervised, will ensure such action.

Materials and Equipment Control

Two distinct aspects of control need to be considered—check-out control and inventory control. The former, which deals with the physical check-out of materials from the center as opposed to the charge-out that precedes it, has been fairly well resolved and proven effective through the installation of electronic detect systems. Many studies have been conducted on loss of materials, so little doubt remains about the cost-effectiveness of a detect system. The installation of such a system has implication for the technical services unit in that the system becomes part of the processing procedure for both materials and equipment. As a general rule, all materials and equipment should be sensitized with the electronic material (or whatever else the system may use), but not if the materials or equipment are such that they cannot be desensitized because of their size or nature. Some items, like documents and pamphlets, may not lend themselves to this system at all on the cost-effective approach and thus should not be so processed. Whatever processing is decided upon as essential and feasible, though, should be worked into the processing routine at the earliest possible time to avoid undue loss of materials and equipment.

Inventories of both materials and equipment are often a function of technical services. It is rather standard at least that the shelf-list, serving as the inventory record of both print and nonprint materials, is maintained and produced there. Routines should be developed carefully and procedures should be monitored to make the shelf-list an accurate on-going record of holdings.

Equipment should be placed on a computer inventory base, and meticulously prepared records should be maintained. Extra precaution should be taken to ensure that the equipment assigned to departments and other units on campus has been so recorded that periodic physical inventories can be taken. Only this type of accuracy will provide reliable records, thereby preventing the disappearance of expensive and indispensible equipment. Inventory may or may not fall into the realm of technical services; but even if it does not, assurance that the original entry into any computer data base is accurate may be the responsibility of either acquisitions or processing.

SUMMARY

The organization of technical services must reflect not only the goals and objectives of the LRC, but also the role expectation held of its personnel in the educational process. Many alternative organization patterns exist if the director is guided, not bound, by traditional approaches. Personnel should be not only well trained within their own specialities, but they should also have a broad, overall view of the entire field of communications. They cannot be disciplined by a preference for a particular format of material, since the collection is built on the concept of an alternative base of ideas regardless of format. Personnel must be open to change and flexible in their work, yet they must adhere to high standards. Today's organization cannot reflect the isolation with which personnel in technical services have traditionally cloaked themselves, especially if personal, academic growth is to be realized through collegial involvement.

Short- and long-range goals should be well defined and developed through a management by objectives approach, and the policies developed to reach these goals should be such that procedures based on sound personnel policies, definitive job descriptions, and constant evaluation can be implemented. The various levels of work should be carried out by persons qualified to do so, and professional help should not be expended on non-professional work.

Technical services personnel and supervisors who are open to change and new developments will keep abreast of the literature in the field. Such works as the annual issue of *Library Resources and Technical Services* summarizing the previous year's work in various areas must be mandatory reading, along with the yearly issues of *Advances in Librarianship, Library Technology Reports*, and any works by recognized leaders in the field. A sound philosophical and theoretical base for practical application grounded in study and professionalism will make the technical services unit and its personnel an integral part of not only the LRC, but also of the academic community.

NOTES

[1] Helen W. Tuttle, "From Cutter to Computer: Technical Services in Academic and Research Libraries," *College and Research Libraries* 37 (Sept. 1976): 423.

[2] Ibid., p. 421.

[3] Doralyn Hickey, "Public and Technical Library Services," in *Essays for Ralph Shaw*, ed. by Norman D. Stevens (Metuchen, NJ: Scarecrow, 1975), p. 183.

[4] Tuttle, "From Cutter to Computer," p. 445.

[5] Hickey, "Public and Technical Library Services," p. 182.

[6] Ibid., p. 183.

[7] Eldred Smith, "The Impact of the Subject Specialist Librarian on the Organization and Structure of the Academic Research Library," in *The Academic Library: Essays in Honor of Guy R. Lyle*, ed. by Evan Farber and Ruth Walling (Metuchen, NJ: Scarecrow, 1974), p. 72.

[8] Evert Volkersz, "Library Organization in Academia: Changes from Hierarchical to Collegial Relationships," in *New Dimensions for Academic Library Service*, ed. by E. J. Josey (Metuchen, NJ: Scarecrow, 1975), p. 77.

[9] Ibid., pp. 80-81.

[10] Hickey, "Public and Technical Library Services," p. 188.

[11] Guy R. Lyle, *The Administration of the College Library*, 4th ed. (New York: H. W. Wilson, 1974), p. 181.

[12] Mary D. Carter, Wallace J. Bonk, and Rose Mary Magrill, *Building Library Collections*, 4th ed. (Metuchen, NJ: Scarecrow, 1974), p. 141.

[13] Ibid., p. 140.

[14] Pearce Grove, ed., *Nonprint Media in Academic Libraries* (Chicago: American Library Association, 1975).

[15] Warren Hicks and Alma Tillin, *Managing Multimedia Libraries* (New York: Bowker, 1977), pp. 163-64.

[16] Tuttle, "From Cutter to Computer," p. 445.

[17] Doris M. Carson, "The Act of Cataloging," *Library Resources and Technical Services* 20 (Spring 1976): 149.

[18] Jesse H. Shera, *Documentation and the Organization of Knowledge* (Hamden, CT: Archon, 1966), pp. 131-32.

[19] Ibid., p. 90.

[20] Paul D. Berrisford, "Year's Work in Cataloging and Classification: 1976," *Library Resources and Technical Services* 21 (Summer 1977): 251.

[21] Ibid., pp. 249-73.

[22] Lyle, *Administration of the College Library*, p. 53.

[23] Hicks and Tillin, *Managing Multimedia Libraries*, pp. 172-73.

[24] Robert S. Taylor, "Innovations in Libraries: Effect on Function and Organization," in *Toward a Theory of Librarianship*, ed. by Conrad Rawski (Metuchen, NJ: Scarecrow, 1973), p. 452.

[25] Ibid., p. 455.

[26] Rutherford D. Rogers and David C. Weber, *University Library Administration* (New York: H. W. Wilson, 1971), pp. 303-317.

[27] J. Michael Bruer, "Resources in 1976," *Library Resources and Technical Services* 21 (Summer 1977): 233.

[28] Barbara E. Markuson, "The Ohio College Library Center System: A Study of Factors Affecting the Adaptation of Libraries to On-Line Networks," *Library Technology Reports* 12 (Jan. 1976): 11-129.

[29] David C. Weber, "A Century of Cooperative Programs Among Academic Libraries," *College and Research Libraries* 37 (May 1976): 205-221.

[30] Ibid., p. 219.

[31] Agnes M. Grady, "Divided Catalogs: A Selected Bibliography," *Library Resources and Technical Services* 20 (Spring 1976): 131-42.

[32] Ibid., p. 140.

[33] Ibid., p. 131.

[34] Donald Foster, *Managing the Catalog Department* (Metuchen, NJ: Scarecrow, 1975), p. 65.

[35] Rogers and Weber, *University Library Administration*, pp. 11-12.

[36] Lyle, *Administration of the College Library*, p. 198.

[37] Barbara A. Rice, "The Development of Working Collections in University Libraries," *College and Research Libraries* 38 (July 1977): 311.

[38] Ibid.

8

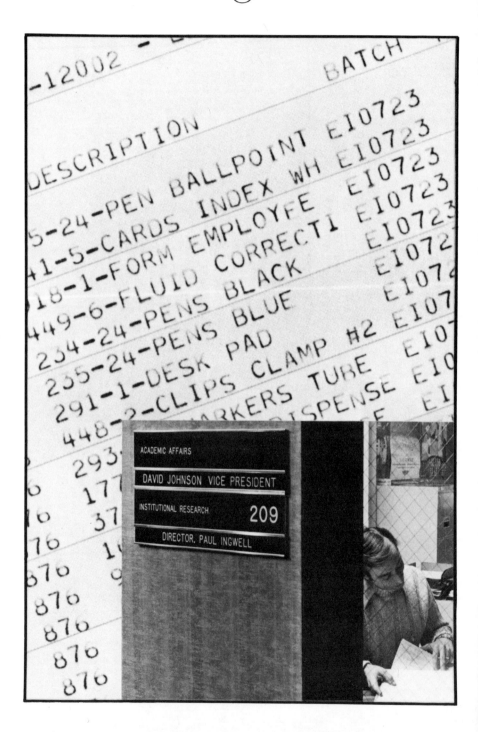

MANAGEMENT, PERSONNEL, AND FINANCE

Before turning to such critical areas as personnel and financing, the authors want to reinforce their commitment to management by objectives (MBO) with a brief analysis of its application. While not devoting any previous section to MBO, the authors have tried to emphasize throughout the necessity of a well-defined management plan based on clearly defined goals and objectives.

MANAGEMENT

MBO as a management technique first became prominent in 1954 when Peter Drucker coined the phrase in his book *The Practice of Management*.[1] Since that time the term has been used and the concept applied with varying amounts of success in government and business, and more recently in libraries. Evans,[2] Hicks and Tillin,[3] and Stueart and Eastlick[4] have all come forth with major works dealing with some aspect of the application of MBO to library management. Hicks and Tillin give not only an excellent verbal account, but they also effectively demonstrate it visually.[5]

Since the concept has been defined, modified, and changed in the literature with relative frequency and with little consistency, it is perhaps imperative that a clear definition be adopted. George Odiorne, in his *Management by Objectives*, has defined MBO as:

> ... a process whereby the superior and subordinate managers of an enterprise jointly identify its common goals, define each individual's major areas of responsibility in terms of the results expected of him and assess the contributions of each of its members.[6]

Bearing that definition in mind, a look at a visual representation of the process becomes helpful as well. The cycle of steps involved in the MBO process can be defined by use of a flow chart; e.g., Hersey and Blanchard[7] used the following chart (Figure 17, page 140) to outline the process.

Figure 17

The MBO Process

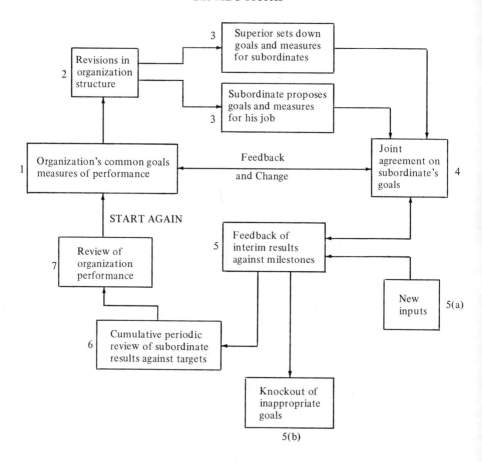

Source: Paul Hersey and Kenneth H. Blanchard, *Management of Organizational Behavior: Utilizing Human Resources.* 2nd ed., ©1972, p. 106. Reprinted by permission of Prentice-Hall, Inc., Englewood Cliffs, New Jersey.

Analysis of the flow chart should make clear MBO's demands that objectives be keyed to both short- and long-range plans, that objectives be clearly stated, and that objectives be measurable rather than vague generalizations. Only such application will produce anticipated results.

A multiplicity of factors appears to account for the evolution of MBO. Among the most evident of these has been the general tightening of the economy and particularly the reduction of funding for higher education; changing attitudes about work relationships; and recognition of the value of professional and skilled employee contributions toward the general organizational function. MBO draws heavily upon the principles set forth in such well-known theories as Maslow's hierarchy of needs, Herzberg's identification of motivators and hygiene factors, McGregor's Theory X and Y, and Likert's participative style of leadership in fostering commitment to objectives.

The implementation of the MBO concept in resource centers should reflect the same improvements experienced in many libraries: improvement in planning; improvement in performance and feedback; increased coordination between and among departments; increased control over the achievement of objectives; and improved flexibility. A more long-range result is an improved superior-subordinate relationship, resulting in staff members seeking more personal development.

A summary statement on management by objectives was clearly stated in a previous work by one of the present authors. In speaking of the humane way of management, Fields concluded:

> Management by objectives for libraries is of paramount importance. Phases of development, planning, organizing, controlling, and measuring are vital. Objectives within each phase or aspect of the organization, combined with the alternatives and the flexibility to incorporate them, are also essential. Total involvement by staff at all levels must be incorporated into any management scheme that intends to be humane and responsive. At a time when major budget cuts loom over almost every facet of public service, accountability is a virtual necessity; the time for a humane system of management by objectives is long overdue.[8]

PERSONNEL

There is little doubt that the most dynamic and vital component of an LRC is its personnel. While a balanced collection of resources and an adequate physical facility are necessary, the staff provides the interface between the resources and the user. Not only is it essential that personnel have quality education and an orientation toward the user, but it is also imperative that they develop and retain positive attitudes toward the combined library and instructional technology program. Personnel must recognize that, in an age of change, they too will need to continue their education and professional growth to be productive members of a vital, lively staff.

With a multiplicity and diversity of services provided within the LRC, it logically follows that personnel must be drawn from a variety of backgrounds; and as the organization expands, expanded services will demand even more specialization with a much greater depth of expertise from individual staff members. Many of the specialists will be drawn from traditionally oriented library and audiovisual personnel; but to become effective members of the LRC staff, each must continually strive to develop both professionally and attitudinally into a competent media person. The prerequisite for development into a media specialist will be a generalist background, for without such an educational foundation, the task of accomplishing the change in attitude from the traditional library to the learning resources concept will be most difficult.

It is clear that if the specialist with a generalist background or, conversely, the generalist with specialist knowledge, cannot be found, then the only remaining course of action is for the LRC to provide an opportunity for staff development. It is suggested that release time be given to those staff members who wish to gain additional competencies in print or nonprint areas, as well as in theory, instructional development, and whatever other needs may develop. The fact that subject specialization may be necessary must also not be overlooked.

Variations existing between traditionally organized library and audiovisual centers and the LRC reflect the fact that the philosophy of the staff, and more important, that of the director or dean of the organization, was of significance.[9] It is important that the directors of LRCs have a clear understanding of the philosophical basis of the learning resources concept, especially if they are to direct such a program without bias toward either the more traditional library and/or audiovisual units.

Ultimately, it seems that the LRC staff in its totality will provide flexibility for the unit because of its great diversity. Staff potential can be realized to its fullest extent and advantage in a learning resource environment. A change in attitude and a commitment to the concept of learning resources is necessary on the part of the staff, or the LRC will be no more successful than the traditional separate library and technology departments. Such a concept is in agreement with the conclusion of John Ellison, who stated that "the nature of the available personnel needed for such a center is critical. Staff must understand and accept the learning resource center concept if it is going to work and work well."[10]

Although there are many programs today that develop a broad background in one area or the other, the quality and the quantity of programs preparing learning resource specialists is still limited. Adequately prepared personnel in the media area are difficult to find, and the attempt to locate individuals who have a desire to expand their talents to work in a thoroughly integrated learning resources program will often lead to frustration. Therefore, it is important to note that staff development will play a significant role in bringing generalist competencies to library and audiovisual specialists. Given time and imagination, a well-qualified staff can be developed through such a program, a measure that will be essential until such time as more institutions realize the demand for media personnel and adjust programs accordingly.

With respect to the competencies necessary to function effectively within the LRC, every administrator should be aware of the statement of policy on *Library Education and Manpower* developed by the American Library Association and published in June 1970. Special attention should be given to Figure 1 in the statement, which recognizes the need for both "library-related" and "non-library related" qualifications. These can be appropriately applied to the LRC. Also of importance is the "Career Lattices" approach (depicted in Figure 2 of the statement), a concept important in utilizing the various skills and talents of LRC staff members.

Personnel Program

Good staff morale is difficult to achieve in the LRC where an attempt is made to provide suitable continuing education conditions for its personnel while, at the same time, maximum performance is expected from them through good staff utilization. In order to maintain good morale, a well-developed personnel program is mandatory, especially when different graduate preparation often leads to misunderstanding or a lack of respect. Even when such a program is mandated by the parent institution, the development of unit criteria will be the major responsibility of the dean and faculty of the LRC. Such a personnel program is usually achieved through developing the following: 1) written job descriptions, 2) a set of written personnel policies relating to such things as appointment, promotion, tenure, etc., and 3) a process for evaluation of job performance.

Job Descriptions

Job descriptions are written statements delineating the responsibilities and tasks expected for a particular position and outlining the relationship of that position to other units in the organization. There is no standard form for job descriptions, but some samples are given in Appendix B. Job descriptions fulfill several important personnel and management needs. They can be used effectively in recruitment as a basis for determining special needs within the organization, and they can also be used as the basis for evaluation of employee performance. Additionally, job descriptions are important in guaranteeing that all employees, regardless of race, color, creed, or sex, are treated equally.

Personnel Policies

Personnel policies in the LRC, if different from those of the parent institution, should be clearly delineated in writing and presented to all personnel at the time of employment. It is important that if tenure and promotion are contingent upon factors other than job performance (i.e., achievement of a number of credits in a field of study, completion of a degree, publication, etc.), then all personnel must be made fully aware of those conditions. In the same way, job descriptions can become personnel policies in that they establish parameters that govern the conditions under which people are expected to perform (i.e., hours, weekend work, position changes, retrenchment, etc.).

Performance Evaluation

Performance evaluation can have implications beyond its role of measuring the efficiency of task fulfillment (and thus how effectively goals and objectives are being met). For purposes of this work, performance measurement should be considered only in light of what performance means to the unit and its goals. It must be remembered that professional responsibilities beyond those delineated in job descriptions are also inherent in performance and are difficult to measure. Use of evaluations to determine merit payments, promotion in rank, appointment, or tenure is not the type of measurement intended here, even though it could ultimately fulfill that purpose for the college administration.

Whatever type of performance measurement is utilized, it should be done in light of job descriptions that are written for every position. It is to be hoped that these will reflect the written goals and objectives of the LRC. Consequently, it matters little whether one of the numerous published evaluation instruments is used or whether the LRC develops its own; but the administrator who wishes to adopt one of the commonly accepted models should refer to Maurice Marchant's *Participative Management in Academic Libraries.*[11]

The methodology used in performance measurement is perhaps as important as the model. Early in the new academic year, each immediate supervisor should meet individually with unit personnel to ensure that both understand precisely what is expected from the person who is to hold a particular position for that year. Periodic, but scheduled, evaluations will be helpful in eliminating misunderstanding or conflicts likely to develop, but the major evaluation should take place at the end of the year and should again involve both the supervisor and the unit employee.

Staffing

As is the case in the traditional library and audiovisual center, three principal staff categories exist in the LRC. The first category consists of the professional staff; the second, of non-professional, supportive or paraprofessional staff; the third, of student assistants. Emphasis in this work will be directed toward the professional category; nevertheless, a few comments about the supportive and student staff categories are imperative.

Student Assistants

Anyone who has worked in a learning resource center, a library, or an audiovisual center is keenly aware that students provide important assistance in these areas. Usually, they perform work of a routine nature—checking out books, transporting equipment, filing catalog cards, assisting with typing and marking, doing bibliographic checking, etc. Administrators certainly must recognize that student assistants cannot replace trained full-time staff, in spite of the fact that in recent years, work-study programs have increased the availability of student help.

Although the tremendous contribution that students make is readily apparent, there are certain disadvantages connected with employing them. Such things as conflicts with scheduled classwork and activities, an important date, the shortness of the employment period, and the employment of a student who lacks motivation to work and would prefer to study are all likely to occur. Despite all these disadvantages, however, students should continue to be employed in the LRC. Their involvement, if treated positively, can assist not only the student but also their LRC colleagues in the development of an attitude that should carry on to their professional and personal lives.

Supportive Staff

Supportive or non-professional staff is often classified as paraprofessional, clerical, and technical staff. The range of expertise in this staff has become ever greater; and now there are not only secretaries and clerks, but other library technicians, media technicians, television engineers, technical engineers, etc. The educational level of these people can also vary greatly. It is generally accepted today that learning resource staff must include adequate support personnel, and this is especially true if the professional staff is to devote attention to non-routine and developmental tasks. The deployment and ratio of nonprofessional/professional staff will, of course, vary depending upon the needs of the individual institution.

Professional Staff

The size of each LRC's professional staff will vary with the philosophy that governs its operation. In looking at the type of individuals needed in an LRC, it seems appropriate to consider personnel functions, which can be divided easily into six functional areas:

1. *Support Function.* The most readily apparent of any library function encompasses basic selection, acquisition, processing, evaluation, and distribution/retrieval routines for materials. Almost any medium, print or non-print, lends itself to library-like routines; and generally, library science curricula adequately prepare individuals for this function. For this reason, it can be assumed that personnel for the support function are readily available from library science programs, and such staff is probably at hand in most centers.

2. *Instructional Function.* With the impact of the statements by the Council on Library Resources and the National Endowment for the Humanities, and the increased activities on campuses in the area of library staff involvement in the educational process, the instructional role of the library and the learning center is becoming more formalized. This suggests a wide variety of activities, both formal and informal, among which are demonstrating instructional research methodology; conducting usage tours of the center; providing in-service workshops for faculty or students on the utilization of media and the production of free and inexpensive materials; and developing training programs for media paraprofessionals and professionals. Personnel in such positions must have a thorough understanding of the learning process and should have had experience in teaching.

3. *Production Function.* Production implies a variety of activities— from producing a booklist, leaflet, or brochure to generating videotape programs, 8mm films, a computer program, or a total learning package encompassing multiple formats. Specialists trained in communications and development skills are essential in order to realize completely the potential of this activity. The necessarily hybrid types of educational technology personnel are being trained in programs throughout the United States.

4. *Administrative Function.* The administrators of the center are usually charged with the responsibility for development. They must be able to identify programs, establish policy, provide responsible direction, and provide cohesion in allocating resources. Such individuals must have a broad understanding of both the traditional library and the audiovisual field, and they must be well versed in learning theory and instructional development as well. A broad understanding of systems analysis and the potential of the LRC are essential in this individual, too.

5. *The Development Function.* Instructional development is the most innovative function of an LRC. The individual who carries out this function should be a trained specialist who has the necessary tools to work with faculty and students in selection, procurement, development and execution of systematically designed learning materials and curricula. In addition, a strong background in learning theory and instructional technology is necessary.

6. *Specialized Functions.* As the LRC grows, and as instructional support services become part of it, the types of functions and the personnel required to fill those specialized roles will increase. Most of the functions of the LRC are highly interrelated and do not always indicate a need for different specialists. For example, larger production centers will demand different specialists for such areas as graphics, photography, audio-video production, motion picture production, television production, computer program design, etc. Ideally, the educator and the learner who utilize the LRC will have all of the center's resources available to them, be they materials, space, personnel, equipment, or any combination of these.

Legal Considerations in Staff Development

The LRC director must become familiar with recent legislation in at least two areas if effective organization is expected to be developed. One of these areas of concern is "affirmative action"; the other is that of employee organizations, which often dictate the conditions under which employees are hired and under which they continue to work.

Equal Opportunity

Efforts to prohibit discrimination in America go back to the Civil Rights Acts of 1866 and 1871, and the Equal Protection Clause of the 14th Amendment of the U.S. Constitution. Affirmative Action was introduced by President Kennedy in 1961 by Executive Order 10925, which established the President's Committee on Equal Employment Opportunity. The Equal Pay Act of 1963 forbids sex discrimination in salaries and benefits in educational institutions and agencies. Title VII of the Civil Rights Act of 1964 prohibits discrimination on the basis of race, religion, national origin, color or sex. Part of Title VII established the Equal Employment Opportunity Commission which is the enforcement agency. Title IX of the 1972 Education Amendments to the Civil Rights Act of 1964 prohibits sex discrimination in the treatment of employees and students at educational institutions that receive grants from the federal government. The Amendments call for an affirmative action plan.[12]

It is imperative that the LRC administration keep current with the laws and regulations governing employment practices. The *Chronicle of Higher Education* is a helpful source as well as the Library Administration Division (LAD) of ALA.

Employee Organizations

Although unionization in libraries began in the early part of the twentieth century, the union movement in libraries is a relatively recent one. On January 8, 1945, the librarians at Howard University organized Local 10, UFWA [United Furniture Workers of America], CIO. The local and the university signed their contract on April 16, 1946, and Howard's was thus the first academic library staff to become unionized. This union, however, was disbanded on June 30, 1950.[13]

It was not until the early 1960s that many academic libraries seriously considered unionization. This move was encouraged by the federal employees having gained the right to bargain collectively with the government, by campus militancy, by the political climate, and by supportive local political forces which emerged during the period. The increased size of library systems also encouraged development of unions in that employees felt they would have a relatively secure base from which to speak on their own behalf. Additionally, Robert Haro speculated in the *ALA Bulletin* that our concepts of employer-employee relationships caused the unionization of librarians. The dual demand for faculty status and an expanded policy-making role in both the library and the academic community have brought about these new concepts.[14]

Generally, unionization of library-media personnel will be dependent on the frequency of unionization of other higher education personnel. The trend within the last five years has definitely been in favor of electing exclusive bargaining agents. Furthermore, as state collective bargaining laws change and state employees are permitted to bargain, there will be an increase in college faculty unionization and, subsequently, among library-media staffs.

In higher educational institutions where libraries are unionized, the three major affiliations are: the American Association of University Professors (AAUP); the American Federation of Teachers (AFT), a part of AFL-CIO; and the National Education Association (NEA). The AAUP has its strongest appeal to research libraries, while NEA is strongest with the historical teachers' colleges and regional institutions. The AFT is considered the most militant of the three and its roots are in the labor movement. The AFT union at the University of California at Berkeley, probably one of the best known of the academic library unions in the country, is discussed in Rogers and Weber.[15] Little doubt remains that the contemporary LRC administrator must keep up to date with the development in this area and should look at library unions as building a better bridge between library administration and staff members.

The staff is the greatest potential resource of any LRC. In the rapidly changing contemporary educational milieu, constant adaptation and modification of roles is required, which further requires greater depth and understanding of the total educational environment. Specialization, with a solid generalist education, is one way in which personnel can be developed who will communicate to those who use the center the soundness of a unified, integrated educational concept of learning resources. A sound personnel program grounded in well-written and well-developed personnel policies should become the backbone of LRC planning. Only then can attention be directed to financial planning.

FINANCES

The statement that the quality of service is almost directly proportional to the quality of the personnel who provide it and the manner in which they do so can hardly be refuted. Without adequate financial support, it is unlikely that even the personnel most vital to quality service can be provided; and even if so, the quality of their work will be severely lowered. Consequently, the level of services will rise and lower just as financial resources do. That is not a hard and fast correlation, but it does emphasize the importance of resources; and if such resources are in short supply, then it strikes at the heart of a good organization.

Before turning to what the authors have labelled systematic financial planning, a look at the evolution of budgeting procedures will provide a framework in which to implement the financial planning proposed.

Budgeting Evolution

The procurement and allocation of money for library operation has always been a primary concern of library administrators. There also has been an increased emphasis within the last few decades on greater accountability for the expenditure of funds. What followed was a greater awareness of the need for better rationale when first requesting funds and a subsequent evaluation in support of further allocations. More stringent control devices have made an appearance, and such phrases as cost benefit analysis, time and motion studies, operations research, and program evaluation and review have become commonplace in the literature. Budget control is a foregone conclusion in most libraries today.

Various budgeting techniques, generally considered on-going and consisting of various stages, are in use today; and the several groups into which they have been classified have been reviewed many times over in the literature. Only a brief attempt will be made here to identify various types of budgeting, and the reader should be cautioned that most budget processes are not usually single, unique systems but rather a combination of the various types available.

The most common and traditional budgeting system used is the "line item." In this type of budget, expenditures are simply divided into broad categories, such as salaries, supplies, capital assets, etc. Yearly increases are based upon a percentage increase over what was allocated the previous year. The major advantage of this system is its simplicity; its greatest disadvantage is probably that it fails to tie expenditures to the objectives of the organization. A variation of the "line item" budget is the approach that allocates a total sum to the library, and the administrators of each unit determine how their portion is to be allocated.

Formula budgets are usually based upon some predetermined standard for allocation. The most popular example is that mentioned in the *Standards for College Libraries*, which states that six percent of the college's total educational and general expenditures should be allocated to the library budget. This type of budgeting certainly has received much of its impetus from the Clapp-Jordan formula,[16] but many other formulas are available.

A newer type of budgeting used in libraries is program budgeting based upon each unit's program. Priorities are not only based upon programs or service but also upon the amount of dollars available. Modification, continuation, or deletion is a function of budget control usually found in such budgets. Closely related is performance budgeting, which places its emphasis on efficient performance of activities. Such a system necessitates careful collection of data and tends to measure quantity of service instead of quality.

Several other budget systems need to be mentioned. Planning Programming Budgeting System (PPBS) combines program and performance budgeting with an emphasis on the planning process. Goals and objectives are established, costs to carry out the goals and objectives are determined, and an evaluation process is identified. Zero-based budgeting is very similar to PPBS in that budgeting is assumed to begin at "zero" each year and allocations are made on the basis of need as determined by assessment and subsequent programming.

Financial Planning

The authors have chosen the broad term financial planning as a label for this vital aspect of management, since they view it as being more than simple budgeting. It is a process consisting of at least five components, of which budgeting is but a part. These components ought to be viewed as stages of a broad process and not necessarily as distinct functions within it. In actuality, the components are characteristic of management by objectives, and without a firm commitment to it, only minimum results can be expected. The five are responsibility, participation, planning, administration, and evaluation. If such terms have a familiar ring to them, then the reader has already recognized a systematic approach. The terminology is hardly important; the concept is. Within this concept, it is quite possible for the administrator to choose any budgeting plan—MBO, PPBS, zero-based budgeting, program budgeting, object budgeting, etc.—and interject it into the planning procedure proposed here.

Responsibility

Many administrators assume that financial planning is a natural process within management, and it is quite evident that, for too many, the process takes its own course with little planning, thus yielding inconsistent results. To manage money without serious regard for eventual results and to accept budget decisions passively is hardly indicative of responsibility.

The effective administrator takes an active responsibility in financial planning through a well-conceived plan based on needs. These needs are, in turn, the basis for securing funds and for judicious allocations. Passive acceptance of funds from the financial officer who makes appropriations based only on past expenditures, or (more likely in today's economy) on a percentage of them, is hardly a substitute for active responsibility based on sound planning. Implied in this responsibility for financial planning is control in all aspects of it—its history, its parameters, its potential—and this type of control should not be construed to mean checks. Rather control ought to be of the type expressed as a requirement by Henri Fayol:

> The control of an undertaking consists of seeing that everything
> is being carried out in accordance with the plan which has been adopted,
> the orders which have been given, and the principles which have been
> laid down.[17]

That is the basis for control, but the authors see it in even a broader context, for it comes about only when the administrator is guided by a comprehensive knowledge of all factors that might affect the process.

Participation

With the advent of planning by objectives, participation has become a by-word. Participation is preceded by responsibility, but no longer only for the director. All members of the LRC staff—professional, clerical, paraprofessional, and technical—must have an active role in any type of financial planning; and responsibility goes hand in hand with participation. All positions carry with them a certain amount of responsibility, and it is only when employees take that responsibility seriously that they become effective members of an organization. The same principle holds true for the financial planning procedure, for *each* must be responsible at their particular level of performance.

Middle management personnel assume an even greater responsibility, but that should be expected, since it would be commensurate with their job responsibilities. People holding such positions will be the basic communication link between the director and personnel in their units; and their recommendations in establishing objectives and priorities and in evaluating become extremely valuable to the director, who makes the final decisions in financial planning.

To the director interested in participative management, such communication is valuable; to financial planning, it is essential. The director may well use such middle-level management techniques as a committee of the whole in order to insure input from all levels. The input from all personnel remains advisory, for, in the final analysis, the director cannot delegate such responsibility, but the alert director will not only seek but also actively use such information.

Planning

This process within the broad financial planning procedure is one that encompasses assignment, writing objectives, setting priorities, budgeting, and evaluating the budget plan. This plan should be based on a systematic approach, regardless of the type of budgeting system used. Since the authors have stressed a management by objectives approach, its application to the budgeting procedure is relatively simple. Hicks and Tillin have placed this in perspective:

> The budget process is really not too difficult in the MBO approach because management, in developing an action plan for a given fiscal period, will have developed a number of objectives that have been articulated in the action plan for the library. Most of these will have fiscal support requirements, and thus become the basis for cost projections in the budget. Cost estimates will then reflect both priority and importance of given objectives.[18]

Comprehensive materials regarding the systems approach in general and its specific applications to library management can be found in many sources. This includes its application to financial planning. LRC directors should not be limited to any particular work, especially with the wealth of materials being published in the area, but the issue of *Library Trends* dealing with "Systems Design and Analysis for Libraries" (April 1973) should be extremely useful. It should be especially helpful for its discussion of the various aspects of systems approaches and the applications thereof.

Systems approaches, while basically the same regardless of the model, are holistic and goal- or objective-oriented, at least in the generic sense. It is a means to management end (or goal), and it must be viewed as such. It does not by itself manage; however, given sound and capable personnel, it can be both a humane and efficient management approach. Systems analysis is generally a linear approach and suggests that operations be analyzed through a series of prescribed steps, starting with problem identification and culminating with evaluation and feedback. Its application to budgeting becomes readily apparent.

Administration

Administration here refers to those procedures necessary for budget approval, expenditure management, and budget alteration during the fiscal year. All are critical if previous planning is to bear fruit, so administration must maintain an air of responsibility.

Nothing can take the place of a knowledgeable and emotionally stable LRC director who approaches institutional superiors with tact, confidence, and preparation. The director should be knowledgeable not only about funding for the LRC, but also about the financial status and budgeting procedures for the entire institution. If there is a likelihood that funds may become available because of cutbacks elsewhere, the director should be intuitive enough to know what to do. Likewise, if unexpected funds from the institution's operational budget become available at year's end, the alert director will be prepared to make judicious use of such funds and to provide a rationale for a share of them. Numerous works on grantmanship are available within the literature, and the alert director who sees state, federal, and private funds as additional revenue knows that they are available.

Expenditure management is good business practice in that it keeps spending within proper limits. Overspending can reduce the director's credibility with her or his immediate superiors, resulting in a lack of confidence in budget preparation. Just as important is the fact that knowing the status of any given account at any particular time can be indicative of progress toward a stated objective, or it can provide exact, immediate expenditure information so as to alleviate fear of over-spending when opportunities for wise expenditure present themselves unexpectedly.

Every budget should have some degree of flexibility built into it. Yet, the director must be cautious in the manipulation of funds lest it interfere with fulfill-ment of objectives. On the other hand, close monitoring of expenditures and observation of progress toward goals might allow the shifting of funds after careful examination in light of objectives. Such alternatives should be given some considera-tion, both in initial planning and as the year progresses.

Evaluation

Evaluation here does not refer to measurement of goals referred to in the sec-tion on budgeting above, but to evaluation of the entire financial planning pro-cedure. If at all possible, financial planning should also be measured against stated goals. In any case, a rigid, thorough introspection in light of the five procedures discussed here should be undertaken.

The confident administrator who is not afraid of constructive criticism may also want to turn to superiors, peers, and subordinates in the evaluation process. While that can be frightening, or even at times demoralizing, it should result in better financial planning, and well-defined, efficient financial planning ought to be the first goal the administrator strives to reach.

Grantsmanship

The availability of federal funds and foundation grants makes it essential that the LRC administrator develop some expertise in grantsmanship. It is necessary to become familiar with such basic sources in the field as *Foundation News, Federal Grant News Monthly, Faculty Alert Bulletin*, and other pamphlets and articles deal-ing with both sources of grants and the "how-to-do-it" of obtaining them. Often, an office on campus is responsible for grant coordination, and its personnel serve as an important resource. Attendance at grants workshops is often money and time well spent and can provide helpful information as well as important contacts.

Financial planning has undergone an evolution from very simple direct line budgeting to a sophisticated PPBS. It has become readily apparent in any organiza-tion that a formal, systematized approach—assessment, establishment of goals and objectives, programming, budgeting, implementation, administration, and evaluation—lies at the heart of efficient allocation and a wise expenditure of funds. The effective LRC administrator provides for participation through responsibility at all levels, not only in planning and administering the financial plan, but also in the evaluation thereof. No system, however, can take the place of an informed administration that takes advantage of its knowledge of financial resources within both the organization and the institution. Proper financial planning, implemented by a confident and tactful administration, will ensure not only access to funds from all sources but also expenditures that will benefit the entire academic community.

SUMMARY

A chapter on management, personnel, and finances would hardly seem complete if it did not include some reference to the interrelation of these three aspects of the LRC. Personnel and finances are without a doubt the lifeblood of the management process, and without either, the LRC cannot adequately serve the academic community and the educational process. The deployment of personnel committed to the learning resources philosophy and highly knowledgeable in all aspects of communication will provide an internal network of efficient and effective services. Exemplary personnel policies, programs, and planning underlie such services. Likewise, the implementation of an effective management by objectives process, properly funded through good financial planning, will allow the LRC to assume its rightful place as the heart of the college or university educational process.

NOTES

[1] Peter F. Drucker, *The Practice of Management* (New York: Harper, 1954).

[2] G. Edward Evans, *Management Techniques for Librarians* (New York: Academic Press, 1976).

[3] Warren B. Hicks and Alma Tillin, *Managing Multimedia Libraries* (New York: Bowker, 1977).

[4] Robert D. Stueart and John Taylor Eastlick, *Library Management* (Littleton, CO: Libraries Unlimited, 1977).

[5] Hicks and Tillin, *Managing Multimedia Libraries*, pp. 110-27.

[6] George S. Odiorne, *Management by Objectives* (New York: Pitman, 1965), p. 4.

[7] Paul Hersey and Kenneth H. Blanchard, *Management of Organizational Behavior*, 2nd ed. (Englewood Cliffs, NJ: Prentice-Hall, 1972).

[8] Dennis C. Fields, "Library Management by Objectives: The Humane Way," *College and Research Libraries* 35 (Sept. 1974): 348.

[9] Dwight F. Burlingame, "A Comparative Study of Organizational Characteristics Used in Learning Resources Centers and Traditionally Organized Library and Audio-Visual Service Facilities in Four Minnesota and Wisconsin Senior Colleges" (Ph.D. dissertation, Florida State University, 1972), p. 59.

[10] John W. Ellison, "An Identification and Examination of Principles Which Validate or Refute the Concept of College or University Learning Resources Centers" (Ph.D. dissertation, The Ohio State University, 1972), p. 221.

[11] Maurice Marchant, *Participative Management in Academic Libraries* (Westport, CT: Greenwood Press, 1976).

[12] U.S. Equal Employment Opportunities Commission, "Affirmative Action and Equal Employment: A Guidebook for Employers," Vol. 1 (Washington: Government Printing Office, 1974), p. 16.

[13] Herbert Biblo, "Librarians and Trade Unionism: A Prologue," *Library Trends* 25 (Oct. 1976): 427.

[14] Robert P. Haro, "Collective Action and Professional Negotiation: Factors and Trends in Academic Libraries," *ALA Bulletin* 63 (July-Aug. 1969): 993.

[15] Rutherford D. Rogers and David C. Weber, *University Library Administration* (New York: H. W. Wilson, 1971), pp. 55-57.

[16] Verner W. Clapp and Robert J. Jordan, "Quantitative Criteria for Adequacy of Academic Library Collections," *College and Research Libraries* 26 (Sept. 1965): 371-80.

[17] Quoted in Stueart and Eastlick, *Library Management*, p. 153.

[18] Hicks and Tillin, *Managing Multimedia Libraries*, p. 118.

APPENDIX A
GUIDELINES FOR THE FORMULATION OF COLLECTION DEVELOPMENT POLICIES

COLLECTION DEVELOPMENT COMMITTEE
Resources Section
Resources and Technical Services Division
American Library Association

THE COLLECTION DEVELOPMENT COMMITTEE of the Resources Section, Resources and Technical Services Division, American Library Association, was organized to provide a focus in ALA for activities relating to collection development, and, in particular, to: study the present resources of American libraries and the coordination of collection development programs; develop guidelines for the definition of selection policies; evaluate and recommend selection tools for collection development; and recommend qualifications and requisite training for selection personnel. In partial response to these charges, the committee at its New York meeting of 9 July 1974 appointed task forces comprised of committee members and consultants to prepare guidelines for the following collection development activities: formula budgeting and allocation; the formulation of collection development policies; the development of review programs designed to assist in the solution of space problems; and the description and evaluation of library collections. The *Guidelines for the Formulation of Collection Development Policies* which follow were prepared by task-force members Thomas Shaughnessy, Hans Weber, and Sheila Dowd (chairman), and were submitted to the committee for revision at its meetings of January and July 1975. They were further revised at the committee's meeting of 19 January 1976 and were then approved for submission to the executive committee of the Resources Section. They were approved as a "preliminary edition" dated March 1976 by the executive committee on 19 July 1976 and were approved by the Board of Directors of RTSD by a mail ballot in August 1976 (seven for publication, one opposed, two not voting).

1. INTRODUCTION

1.1 **Purpose.**
The committee offers these *Guidelines for the Formulation of Collection Development Policies* in the belief that collection develop-

Manuscript received and accepted for publication July 1976.

Source: Reprinted by permission of the American Library Association from "Guidelines for the Formulation of Collection Development Policies," *Library Resources and Technical Services*, Winter 1977, pp. 40-47.

ment policy statements must be comprehensible, and that they must be comparable, particularly if they are to prove useful in the implementation of long-range goals for sharing of resources.

1.2 Objectives.

The immediate aims of the designers of these *Guidelines* are, to identify the essential elements of a written statement of collection development policy, and to establish standard terms and forms for use in the preparation of such policies.

1.3 Need.

Widespread budgetary constraints and the growth of interlibrary cooperation in resources-sharing call for analysis of collection activity in universally comprehensible terms.

1.4 Scope.

The committee has attempted to provide an instrument that will be of use to libraries of all kinds and sizes in formulating statements of their collection development policies. Some elements of the *Guidelines*, however, will of necessity be more applicable to larger libraries.

1.5 Audience.

The *Guidelines* are intended to help library administrators and collection development librarians to produce a document that can serve as both a planning tool and a communications device. The resulting policy statements should clarify collection development objectives to staff, users, and cooperating institutions, enabling them to identify areas of strength in library collections; and by this means should facilitate the coordination of collection development and cooperative services within an area or region.

1.6 Methodology.

The *Guidelines* have been submitted to the committee in open meeting at several Midwinter and Annual Conferences. The group discussions, in which numerous visitors have participated, have resulted in extensive revisions of the initial drafts.

1.7 Assumptions.

1.7.1 A written collection development policy statement is for any library a desirable tool, which: (a) enables selectors to work with greater consistency toward defined goals, thus shaping stronger collections and using limited funds more wisely; (b) informs users, administrators, trustees and others as to the scope and nature of existing collections, and the plans for continuing development of resources; (c) provides information which will assist in the budgetary allocation process.

1.7.2 It is desirable that form and terminology of collection development policy statements be sufficiently standardized to permit comparison between institutions.

1.7.3 Libraries have acknowledged the impossibility of building totally comprehensive collections, and will increasingly need to rely on cooperative activities. Collection development policy statements will assist cooperative collection building, and will also, in the absence of precise bibliographic tools such as union catalogs, be of value to users and user-service units in locating materials.

1.8 Definitions.

    1.8.1 Levels of collection density and collecting intensity codes. The codes defined below are designed for use in identifying both the extent of existing collections in given subject fields (collection density) and the extent of current collecting activity in the field (collecting intensity).

      A. Comprehensive level. A collection in which a library endeavors, so far as is reasonably possible, to include all significant works of recorded knowledge (publications, manuscripts, other forms), in all applicable languages, for a necessarily defined and limited field. This level of collecting intensity is that which maintains a "special collection"; the aim, if not the achievement, is exhaustiveness.

      B. Research level. A collection which includes the major source materials required for dissertations and independent research, including materials containing research reporting, new findings, scientific experimental results, and other information useful to researchers. It also includes all important reference works and a wide selection of specialized monographs, as well as a very extensive collection of journals and major indexing and abstracting services in the field.

      C. Study level. A collection which is adequate to support undergraduate or graduate course work, or sustained independent study; that is, which is adequate to maintain knowledge of a subject required for limited or generalized purposes, of less than research intensity. It includes a wide range of basic monographs, complete collections of the works of more important writers, selections from the works of secondary writers, a selection of representative journals, and the reference tools and fundamental bibliographical apparatus pertaining to the subject.

      D. Basic level. A highly selective collection which serves to introduce and define the subject and to indicate the varieties of information available elsewhere. It includes major dictionaries and encyclopedias, selected editions of important works, historical surveys, important bibliographies, and a few major periodicals in the field.

      E. Minimal level. A subject area which is out of scope for the library's collections, and in which few selections are made beyond very basic reference tools.

      Note: Definitions of collecting levels are not to be applied in a relative or ad hoc manner (that is, relative to a given library or group of libraries) but in a very objective manner. Consequently it is quite likely that a large number of libraries will not hold comprehensive collections in any area. Similarly, academic libraries which do not support doctoral programs, or other types of libraries which are not oriented toward specialized research, may not have any collections that would fall within the research level as defined herein.

The definitions are proposed to describe a range and diversity of titles and forms of material; they do not address the question of availability of multiple copies of the same title.

1.8.2 Language codes.

The following codes should be used to indicate languages in which material is collected. Libraries wishing a greater refinement of this data may sub-code with the MARC language codes.

F. All applicable languages (i.e., no exclusions)
G. English
H. Romance languages
J. Germanic languages
K. Slavic languages
L. Middle Eastern languages
M. Asian languages
N. African languages
P. Other languages

2. GUIDELINES

2.1 Principles governing formulation and application of collection development policies.

2.1.1 Libraries should identify the long- and short-range needs of their clientele, and establish priorities for the allocation of funds to meet those needs. A collection development policy statement is an orderly expression of those priorities as they relate to the development of library resources.

Note: The collection development policy statement addresses the question of breadth and depth of subject coverage. Libraries will need to formulate separate statements of policy relating to duplication of materials; and such additional policy statements must be given consideration in fund allocation.

2.1.2 Collection development policy statements should be reviewed at regular intervals to insure that changes in user needs are recognized, and that changing budgetary situations are confronted.

2.1.3 A library's collection development policy should be coordinated with those of appropriate other libraries, whether in a hierarchy of dependence, or in a division of responsibility among equals. A collection development policy statement should assist librarians to select and de-select in conformity with regional needs and resources.

2.2 Elements of a collection development policy statement.

    2.2.1 Analysis of general institutional objectives, including:

        (1) Clientele to be served

        (2) General subject boundaries of the collection

        (3) Kinds of programs or user needs supported (research, instructional, recreational, general information, reference, etc.)

        (4) General priorities and limitations governing selection, including:

            (a) degree of continuing support for strong collections

            (b) forms of material collected or excluded

            (c) languages, geographical areas collected or excluded

            (d) chronological periods collected or excluded

            (e) other exclusions

            (f) duplication of materials (generally treated; but see also 2.1.1, Note)

        (5) Regional, national, or local cooperative collection agreements which complement or otherwise affect the institution's policy.

    2.2.2 Detailed analysis of collection development policy for subject fields. The basic arrangement of this analysis is by classification; a parenthetical subject term follows the class number for ease of interpretation. A suggested minimum of refinement of the Library of Congress classification on which to structure the analysis is the breakdown into approximately 500 subdivisions used in: *Titles Classified by the Library of Congress Classification: Seventeen University Libraries.* Preliminary ed. Berkeley, General Library, University of California, 1973. (A list of the classes used in that survey is appended to these guidelines.) For Dewey or other classifications, a comparably refined breakdown should be attempted.

        Note: This recommendation indicates a minimal refinement of classification analysis needed to permit interinstitutional comparisons. Many libraries will prefer to analyze their collections in greater detail.

    For each subject category (i.e., classification number or group of numbers), indicate the following:

    (1) Level of collecting intensity codes to indicate:

        (a) existing strength of collection

        (b) actual current level of collection activity

        (c) desirable level of collecting to meet program needs

(2) Language code or codes
(3) Chronological periods collected
(4) Geographical areas collected
(5) Forms of material collected (or excluded)
(6) Library unit or selector with primary selection responsibility for the field

2.2.3 Detailed analysis of collection development policy for form collections.

In some libraries special collection development policy statements are required for certain forms of materials, where policy governing the collection of those materials differs from the library's general policy for subject collections. Some examples of forms for which special policy statements may be needed include:

(1) Newspapers
(2) Microform collections
(3) Manuscripts
(4) Government publications
(5) Maps
(6) Audio-visual materials
(7) Data tapes

Where possible, it is desirable that the basic structure of the policy statement for a form collection follow subject classification; but with some form collections it will be necessary to use another primary arrangement (kind of material, area, etc.). For example, the policy statement for a map collection might be divided first into "general maps," "topographic maps," "thematic maps," "raised relief maps," etc., with subdivision by area classification; that for a newspaper collection might be primarily by political division.

Whatever the basic structure chosen, the detailed analysis of collection development for a form collection should include the elements identified in 2.2.2 (1) – (6) above.

2.2.4 Indexes.

The information in the policy statement should be made accessible for a wide variety of purposes. To this end an index should be appended which correlates subject terms to class numbers. Individual libraries may also wish to index by academic programs, library units, or other key words or concepts.

APPENDIX

Classes used in *Titles Classified by the Library of Congress Classification: Seventeen University Libraries*

AC	AI	AP	AZ
AF	AM	AS	B1–68
AG	AN	AY	B69–789

B790–5739	F1–205	JQ	PF3001–5999
BC	F206–475	JS	PG1–489
BD	F476–705	JV1–5399	PG500–585
BF1–1000	F721–854	JV6001–9500	PG601–799
BF1001–1400	F856–975	JX	PG801–1158
BF1401–1999	F1000–1170	K–KE	PG1161–1164
BH	F1201–1392	KF	PG1171–1798
BJ1–1800	F1401–1419	KFA–KFW	PG1801–1998
BJ1801–2195	F1421–1577	KFX	PG2900–3155
BL	F1601–2151	L	PG3200–3299
BM	F2161–2175	LA	PG3300–3490
BP	F2201–3799	LB	PG3500–3560
BR	G1–890	LC	PG3801–3998
BS	G1001–3102	LD	PG4001–5198
BT	G3160–9980	LE	PG5201–5598
BV	GA1–87	LF	PG5631–5698
BX1–799	GA100–1999	LG	PG6001–7498
BX800–4795	GB	LH	PG7900–7948
BX4800–9999	GC	LJ	PG8001–9268
C	GF	LT	PG9501–9678
CB	GN1–295	M1–4	PH1–79
CC	GN307–686	M5–1490	PH91–498
CD	GN700–875	M1495–5000	PH501–1109
CE	GR	ML	PH1201–3718
CJ	GT	MT	PH5001–5490
CN	GV1–198	N	PJ1–995
CR	GV201–553	NA	PJ1001–1989
CS	GV557–1197	NB	PJ2001–2199
CT	GV1200–1570	NC	PJ2301–2551
D1–900	GV1580–1799	ND	PJ3001–4091
D901–1075	GV1800–1860	NE	PJ4101–5809
DA	H	NK	PJ5901–9288
DB	HA	NX	PK1–90
DC	HB	P	PK101–2891
DD	HC	PA1–2995	PK2901–5534
DE	HD1–100	PA3000–3049	PK6001–6599
DF	HD101–1395	PA3050–4500	PK6701–6996
DG	HD1401–2210	PA5000–5665	PK7001–9601
DH	HD2321–4730	PA6000–7041	PL1–489
DJ	HD4801–8942	PA8001–8595	PL490–495
DK	HE	PB1–431	PL501–898
DL	HF1–4050	PB1001–3029	PL901–998
DP1–500	HF5001–6351	PC1–400	PL1001–3299
DP501–900	HG	PC601–872	PL3301–3505
DQ	HJ	PC890	PL3521–4587
DR	HM	PC901–986	PL4601–4961
DS1–40	HN	PC1001–1984	PL5001–7101
DS41–329	HQ	PC2001–3761	PL7501–7893
DS330–500	HS	PC3801–3976	PL8000–8844
DS501–935	HT	PC4001–4977	PM1–95
DT	HV	PC5001–5498	PM101–7356
DU	HX	PD1–777	PM7801–7895
DX	J	PD1001–1350	PM8001–9021
E1–139	JA	PD1501–7159	PN1–44
E140–200	JC	PE	PN45–75
E201–299	JF	PF1–979	PN80–99
E301–440	JK	PF1001–1184	PN101–249
E441–655	JL	PF1401–1558	PN441–1009
E656–859	JN		PN1010–1588

PN1600–1657	PR1–78	QC221–246	S1–760
PN1660–1864	PR81–151	QC251–338	S900–972
PN1865–1989	PR161–479	QC350–496	SB
PN1991–1992	PR500–978	QC501–798	SD
PN1993–1999	PR1098–1395	QC801–999	SF
PN2000–2081	PR1490–1799	QD1–69	SH
PN2085–2219	PR1803–2165	QD71–145	SK
PN2220–2298	PR2199–2405	QD146–199	T
PN2300–2554	PR2411–2416	QD241–449	TA
PN2570–2859	PR2417–2749	QD450–731	TC
PN2860–3030	PR2750–3112	QD901–999	TD
PN3035	PR3135–3198	QE	TE
PN3151–3191	PR3291–3785	QH1–199	TF
PN3195–3300	PR3991–5990	QH201–278	TG
PN3311–3503	PR6000–6049	QH301–705	TH
PN4001–4355	PR6050–6076	QK1–474	TJ
PN4390–4500	PR8309–9899	QK475–989	TK
PN4699–5650	PS1–478	QL1–355	TL
PN6010–6078	PS501–690	QL362–739	TN
PN6080–6095	PS700–893	QL750–991	TP
PN6099–6120	PS991–3390	QM	TR
PN6121–6146	PS3500–3549	QP1–348	TS
PN6147–6231	PS3550–3576	QP351–499	TT
PN6233–6381	PT1–951	QP501–801	TX
PN6400–6525	PT1100–1485	QP901–981	U
PQ1–841	PT1501–1695	QR	UA
PQ1100–1297	PT1701–1797	R1–130	UB
PQ1300–1595	PT1799–2592	R131–687	UC
PQ1600–1709	PT2600–2659	R690–899	UD
PQ1710–1935	PT2660–2688	RA3–420	UE
PQ1947–2147	PT3701–4899	RA421–790	UF
PQ2149–2551	PT5001–5395	RA791–955	UG
PQ2600–2651	PT5400–5547	RA960–998	UH
PQ2660–2686	PT5555–5880	RA1001–1171	V
PQ3800–3999	PT5881	RA1190–1270	VA
PQ4001–4263	PT5885–5980	RB	VB
PQ4265–4556	PT6000–6471	RC1–106	VC
PQ4561–4664	PT6500–6590	RC110–253	VD
PQ4675–4734	PT6592	RC254–298	VE
PQ4800–4886	PT7001–7099	RC306–320	VF
PQ5901–5999	PT7101–7599	RC321–431	VG
PQ6001–6269	PT7601–8260	RC435–576	VK
PQ6271–6498	PT8301–9155	RC578–632	VM
PQ6500–6576	PT9201–9999	RC633–935	Z4–15
PQ6600–6647	PZ1–4	RC936–951	Z40–115
PQ6651–6676	PZ5–10	RC952–1299	Z116–550
PQ7000–7079	PZ11–99	RD	Z551–661
PQ7080–7087	Q	RE	Z662–1000
PQ7100–7349	QA1–99	RF	Z1001–1121
PQ7361–7539	QA101–145	RG	Z1201–1212
PQ7551–8560	QA150–299	RJ	Z1215–1361
PQ8600–8929	QA300–433	RK	Z1365–1401
PQ9000–9189	QA440–699	RL	Z1411–1945
PQ9191–9255	QA801–939	RM	Z2000–2959
PQ9261–9288	QB	RS	Z3001–4980
PQ9400–9479	QC1–75	RT	Z5051–5055
PQ9500–9696	QC81–119	RV	Z5056–8999
PQ9697–9699	QC120–168	RX	
PQ9900–9999	QC170–220	RZ	

APPENDIX B
SAMPLE JOB DESCRIPTIONS FOR LRC POSITIONS

POSITION DESCRIPTION NO. 1—St. Cloud State University, May 3, 1976

Learning Resources Services *and* Department of Library and Audiovisual Education—Production Services

Position Title: Photo Assistant

Reports To: Dennis C. Fields, Supervisor, Production Services Division, and Lawrence Smelser, Supervisor, Instructional Services Division.

Position Purpose: Classroom instruction 15%; Service 85%. The position encompasses the following:

1. Maintain operation of the photographic laboratory with regard to:
    a. supervision of work study students and graduate assistants.
    b. quality control of materials produced.
    c. contribution to completion of faculty requested materials.
    d. ongoing analysis, evaluation, and reorganization, when necessary, of photographic laboratories, procedures, and development efforts.
2. Assist in instructional design and development efforts.
3. Participation in the Instructional Services program—advising and instruction.
4. Develop and produce 8mm and 16mm motion picture projects. (1975-76 Program Review indicates a future service as limited motion picture projects. "Limited" is here defined as approximately one [1] 16mm motion picture per year.)

* * *

POSITION DESCRIPTION NO. 2—St. Cloud State University, May 3, 1976

Learning Resources Services *and* Department of Library and Audiovisual Education

Position Title: Acquisition/Bibliography—Receiving, Binding, and Pro-
                          cessing Section Leader *and* Teaching faculty in the Depart-
                          ment of Library & Audiovisual Education

Reports To: Division Leader, Technical Services Division *and* Division
                          Leader, Advising & Instruction Division.

Position Purpose: This position is accountable for supervising the acquisi-
                          tions, receiving, and processing of print and non-print mate-
                          rials for Learning Resources Services.

Duties and Responsibilities:

General Duties: (Classroom Instruction 20%; Services 80%)

1. To supervise and plan the orderly flow of work within the section.
2. To train and supervise clerk-typists to perform their specific job routines
    within the acquisitions, receiving, and materials processing areas.
3. To identify, select, and acquire instructional materials for the clientele
    served by St. Cloud State University.
4. To account for and to maintain accurate budget records for materials pur-
    chased and for bindery costs.
5. To assign and supervise job routines for student workers employed within the
    section.
6. To establish and supervise the purchasing, accounting, and retrieval procedures
    for periodicals.
7. To perform formal teaching assignments in the Department of Library and
    Audiovisual Education.
8. To coordinate section responsibilities with all areas within Learning Resources
    Services.
9. To perform direct and indirect services to all faculty, students and others
    regarding the acquisitions, receiving, and processing of individual requested
    material.
10. To identify and preview non-print materials and to coordinate the preview
    of these materials with the faculty of St. Cloud State University.
11. To provide general education advisory services.
12. To perform other assignments such as reference and readers' advisory services
    when called upon.

* * *

POSITION DESCRIPTION NO. 3–University of Evansville, July 1, 1977

Title: Dean of Learning Resources

Faculty Rank

Purpose and Scope:

The dean, under the general supervision of the Vice President of Academic Affairs, is responsible for the administration of the library and learning resources unit of the University. Responsibility for general academic policy is shared with the other deans via the Dean's Council.

The dean of learning resources is expected to maintain control of the learning resource system, to communicate effectively with the academic community–its purpose and goals, and to represent the University in the professional and local community in matters relating to Learning Resource Centers.

Principal Responsibilities:

1. To develop policies, services, and resources to meet the immediate and long-range goals the learning resources and the academic community.

2. To plan, organize, implement, and evaluate the library and learning resources operation.

3. To employ effective management techniques in directing, planning, organizing, staffing, coordinating, budgeting, and evaluating the library and learning resources operation.

4. To analyze on a continual basis relevant influencing factors, such as the legal, physical and statistical aspects and their effect on the library and learning resources operation.

5. To provide open avenues for the critical review of library and learning resources operations, such as acquisitions, circulation, personnel management, CIS, and financial administration.

6. To direct the administration of personnel regulations and the review of staff performance, and to approve new staff appointments, promotions, and dismissals.

7. To direct investigation of new trends in specific library and learning resources programs and to facilitate testing of new techniques, materials and equipment for improvement of the operational function.

(Position Description No. 3 continues on page 166.)

POSITION DESCRIPTION NO. 3—University of Evansville, July 1, 1977 (cont'd)

8. To serve as the official representative of the library and learning resource system.

9. To direct the administration of a library and learning resources in-service training program, and to provide for the continuous upgrading of personnel through the encouragement of continuing education.

10. To encourage faculty participation in professional societies, associations, and activities at all levels.

Requirements:

Education: Advanced education in library and educational technology. Ph.D. is preferred. A minimum of 3 years of professional experience with administrative responsibility in a college library or learning resource center.

* * *

ADDITIONAL REFERENCES

CHAPTER 1—THE COLLEGE COMMUNITY

Boyle, Deirdre. "Libraries and Media." *Library Journal* 101 (Jan. 1, 1976): 125-29.

Edelman, Hendrik. "Redefining the Academic Library." *Library Journal* 101 (Jan. 1, 1976): 53-56.

Garbarino, J. W. *Faculty Bargaining*. New York: McGraw-Hill, 1975.

Hicks, Warren B., and Alma M. Tillin. *Managing Multimedia Libraries*. New York: Bowker, 1977.

Kemerer, R. R., and J. V. Baldridge. *Unions on Campus*. San Francisco: Jossey-Bass, 1977.

Knowles, Asa S. *Handbook of College and University Administration*. New York: McGraw-Hill, 1970.

Ladd, Everett Carll, and Seymour Martin Lipset. *The Divided Academy: Professors and Politics*. New York: McGraw-Hill, 1975.

Sanford, Nevitt, ed. *The American College: A Psychological and Social Interpretation of the Higher Learning*. New York: John Wiley, 1962.

Sanford, Nevitt, ed. *College and Character: A Briefer Version of The American College*. New York: John Wiley, 1964.

Shera, Jesse. *Introduction to Library Science: Basic Elements of Library Service*. Littleton, CO: Libraries Unlimited, 1976.

CHAPTER 2—THE PHILOSOPHY OF THE LEARNING RESOURCE CENTER

Brown, James W. *New Media and Public Libraries: A Survey of Current Practices*. New York: Jeffrey Norton, 1976.

Dougherty, Richard M. "The Unserved—Academic Library Style." *American Libraries* 2 (Nov. 1971): 1055-58.

Drucker, Peter F. *The Practice of Management*. New York: Harper, 1954.

Emery, Richard. "Philosophy, Purpose and Function in Librarianship." *Library Association Record* 73 (July 1971): 127-29.

The Formulation and Use of Goals and Objectives in Academic and Research Libraries. Occasional Paper No. 3, Office of University Library Management Studies. Washington: Association of Research Libraries, 1972.

Freedman, Morris. "Integrated School Resource Programs: A Conceptual Framework and Description." *Audiovisual Instruction* 20 (Sept. 1975): 5-9.

McBeath, Ron J. "Program Planning and Management in Audiovisual Services for Higher Education." *Audiovisual Instruction* 16 (Oct. 1971): 62-67.

Media Programs: District and School. Prepared jointly by the American Association of School Librarians, American Library Association, and Association for Educational Communications and Technology. Chicago: ALA; Washington: AECT, 1975.

Orne, Jerrold. "The Undergraduate Library." *Library Journal* 95 (June 15, 1970): 2230-33.

Perkins, John W., et al. *Library Objectives, Goals, and Activities.* Inglewood, CA: Inglewood Public Library, 1973.

Peterson, Gary T. "Conceptualizing the Learning Center." *Audiovisual Instruction* 18 (March 1973): 67.

Prostano, Emanuel T., and Joyce S. Prostano. *The School Library Media Center.* 2nd ed. Littleton, CO: Libraries Unlimited, 1977.

CHAPTER 3—ADMINISTRATIVE ORGANIZATION

Dunlap, Connie R. "Organizational Patterns in Academic Libraries, 1876-1976." *College and Research Libraries* 37 (Sept. 1976): 395-407.

Josey, E. J., ed. *New Dimensions for Academic Library Service.* Metuchen, NJ: Scarecrow, 1975.

Liesener, James W. *A Systematic Process for Planning Media Programs.* Chicago: American Library Association, 1976.

Metz, Paul. "The Academic Library and Its Director in Their Institutional Environments." Ph.D. dissertation, University of Michigan, 1977.

Reynolds, Michael M., ed. *Reader in the Academic Library.* Washington: NCR Microcard Editions, 1971.

Rogers, Rutherford D., and David C. Weber. *University Library Administration.* New York: H. W. Wilson, 1971.

Taylor, Robert S. *The Making of a Library: The Academic Library in Transition.* New York: Hayes and Becker Information Science Service, 1972.

CHAPTER 4–RESOURCES AND INFORMATION

Brown, James, Kenneth Norberg, and Sara Srygley. *Administering Educational Media: Instructional Technology and Library Services.* 2nd ed. New York: McGraw-Hill, 1972.

Buckland, Michael. *Book Availability and the Library User.* New York: Pergamon Press, 1975.

Burlingame, Dwight. *Selection and Evaluation of Media Materials.* New York: MSS Information Corporation, 1973.

Carter, Mary D., Wallace J. Bonk, and Rose Mary Magrill. *Building Library Collections.* 4th ed. Metuchen, NJ: Scarecrow, 1974.

Cheney, Frances N. *Fundamental Reference Sources.* Chicago: American Library Association, 1971.

Cowley, John. *Libraries in Higher Education: The User Approach to Service.* Hamden, CT: Linnet, 1975.

Dillon, Howard. "Organizing the Academic Library for Instruction." *Journal of Academic Librarianship* 1 (Sept. 1975): 4-7.

Grove, Pearce S., ed. *Nonprint Media in Academic Libraries.* Chicago: American Library Association, 1975.

Katz, William. *Introduction to Reference Work. Vol. II: Reference Services and Reference Processes.* 2nd ed. New York: McGraw-Hill, 1974.

Knapp, Patricia B. *College Teaching and the College Library.* ACRL Monograph No. 23. Chicago: American Library Association, 1959.

Knapp, Patricia B. *The Monteith College Experiment.* New York: Scarecrow, 1966.

Lyle, Guy R. *The Administration of the College Library*, 4th ed. New York: H. W. Wilson, 1974.

Lynch, Mary Jo. "Academic Library Reference Policy Statements." *RQ* 11 (Spring 1972): 222-26.

McElderry, Stanley. "Readers and Resources: Public Services in Academic and Research Libraries, 1876-1976." *College and Research Libraries* 37 (Sept. 1976): 408-420.

Miller, Lawrence. "Liaison Work in the Academic Library." *RQ* 16 (Spring 1977): 213-15.

Rader, Hannelore B., ed. *Faculty Involvement in Library Instruction.* Ann Arbor, MI: Pierian Press, 1976.

Rogers, Rutherford, and David Weber. *University Library Administration.* New York: H. W. Wilson, 1971.

Saracenic, T., W. M. Shaw, and P. B. Kantor. "Causes and Dynamics of User Frustration in an Academic Library." *College and Research Libraries* 38 (Jan. 1977): 7-18.

Taylor, Robert S. *The Making of a Library: The Academic Library in Transition.* New York: Hayes and Becker Information Science Service, 1972.

CHAPTER 5–INSTRUCTIONAL TECHNOLOGY SERVICES

Brown, James W., Richard B. Lewis, and Fred H. Harcleroad. *A/V Instruction: Technology, Media, and Methods.* 5th ed. New York: McGraw-Hill, 1977.

Bullough, Robert V. *Creating Instructional Materials.* 2nd ed. Columbus, OH: Charles E. Merrill, 1978.

College Learning Resources Programs. Washington: AECT, 1977.

Davies, Ivor K. *Competency Based Learning: Technology, Management, and Design.* New York: McGraw-Hill, 1973.

Kemp, Jerrold E. *Planning and Producing Audiovisual Materials.* 3rd ed. New York: Thomas Y. Crowell, 1975.

Minor, Edward O. *Handbook for Preparing Visual Media.* 2nd ed. New York: McGraw-Hill, 1978.

Minor, Edward O., and Harvey R. Frye. *Techniques for Producing Visual Instructional Media.* 2nd ed. New York: McGraw-Hill, 1977.

Morlan, John E. *Preparation of Inexpensive Teaching Materials.* 2nd ed. New York: Chandler Publishing Company, 1973.

Wiman, Raymond V. *Instructional Materials.* Worthington, OH: Charles A. Jones Publishing Company, 1972.

CHAPTER 6–INSTRUCTIONAL DEVELOPMENT AND FACULTY DEVELOPMENT

Baker, Robert L., and Richard E. Schutz. *Instructional Product Development.* New York: Van Nostrand Reinhold, 1971.

Bergquist, William H., and Steven R. Phillips. *A Handbook for Faculty Development.* Washington: Council for the Advancement of Small Colleges, 1975.

Bretz, Rudy. *A Taxonomy of Communication Media.* Englewood Cliffs, NJ: Educational Technology Publications, 1971.

Davis, Robert H., Lawrence T. Alexander, and Stephen L. Yelon. *Learning System Design, An Approach to the Improvement of Instruction.* New York: McGraw-Hill, 1974.

Davies, Ivor K. *Objectives in Curriculum Design.* New York: McGraw-Hill, 1976.

Diamond, Robert, et al. *Instructional Development for Individualized Learning in Higher Education.* Englewood Cliffs, NJ: Educational Technology Publications, 1975.

Gagne, Robert M., and Leslie J. Briggs. *Principles of Instructional Design.* New York: Holt, Rinehart and Winston, 1974.

Gale, Fred L. *Determining the Requirements for the Design of Learned-Based Instruction.* Columbus, OH: Charles E. Merrill Publishing Company, 1975.

Levinson, D. J., C. M. Darrow, E. B. Klein, M. H. Levinson, and D. McKee. *The Psychosocial Development of Men in Early Adulthood and the Mid-Life Transition.* In D. F. Ricks, A. Thomas, and M. Roff, eds. *Psychopathology,* Vol. 3. Minneapolis: University of Minnesota Press, 1974.

National Special Media Institutes. *The Affective Domain.* Washington: Gryphon House, 1972.

National Special Media Institutes. *The Cognitive Domain.* Washington: Gryphon House, 1972.

National Special Media Institutes. *The Psychomotor Domain.* Washington: Gryphon House, 1972.

CHAPTER 7–TECHNICAL SERVICES

Gore, Daniel, ed. *Farewell to Alexandria.* Westport, CT: Greenwood Press, 1976.

Lancaster, F. W. *The Measurement and Evaluation of Library Services.* Washington: Information Resources, 1977.

Salmon, Stephen R. *Library Automation Systems.* New York: Marcel Dekker, 1975.

Tillin, Alma M., and William J. Quinly. *Standards for Cataloging Nonprint Materials: An Interpretation and Practical Application.* Washington: Association for Educational Communications and Technology, 1976.

CHAPTER 8–MANAGEMENT, PERSONNEL, AND FINANCE

Chisholm, Margaret E., and Donald P. Ely. *Media Personnel in Education: A Competency Approach.* Englewood Cliffs, NJ: Prentice-Hall, 1976.

Guyton, Theodore Lewis. *Unionization: The Viewpoint of Librarians.* Chicago: American Library Association, 1975.

Lancaster, F. W. *The Measurement and Evaluation of Library Services.* Washington: Information Resources Press, 1977.

Shaughnessy, Thomas W. "Participative Management, Collective Bargaining, and Professionalism." *College and Research Libraries* 38 (March 1977): 140-46.

Weatherford, John W. *Collective Bargaining and the Academic Librarian.* Metuchen, NJ: Scarecrow, 1976.

AUTHOR, TITLE, SUBJECT INDEX